Social Authorship
and the
Advent of Print

Social Authorship
and the
Advent of Print

Margaret J. M. Ezell

The Johns Hopkins
University Press

Baltimore &
London

© 1999 The Johns Hopkins University Press
All rights reserved. Published 1999
Printed in the United States of America
on acid-free paper

2 4 6 8 9 7 5 3 1

The Johns Hopkins University Press
2715 North Charles Street
Baltimore, Maryland 21218-4363
www.press.jhu.edu

Library of Congress Cataloging-in-Publication
Data will be found at the end of this book.

A catalog record for this book is available
from the British Library.

ISBN 0-8018-6139-X

For two of my favorite authors: my father, John S. Ezell,
the rough drafts of whose books provided me with coloring paper
and who later let me use his typewriter to write stories,
and my husband, Jürgen Mainzer, who is just beginning
a new career as an author

Contents

Acknowledgments

Many people have helped to make the research and production of this book a pleasure. Jeffrey Cox and Elizabeth Hageman read early efforts with their usual shrewd and penetrating eyes. Elizabeth Hageman and Nathan Tinker also generously shared their compendious knowledge about Katherine Philips with me. Elsie Duncan-Jones encouraged my interest in manuscript studies and social authors while I was a graduate student, and not long afterwards, many years ago before this project was ever even conceived, Howard Erskine-Hill and J. Paul Hunter shared with me information about Pope's existing manuscripts. Peter Beal has been, as always, an invaluable source of information and encouragement. Devoney Looser provided the opportunity for me to present the preliminary version of one of the chapters at Indiana State University as the Joseph S. Schick Lecture. Arthur Marotti likewise has created a series of excellent forums for the exploration of issues about manuscript culture, a field his own research has helped to define. Donald R. Dickson, Sally Moreman, Charles Snodgrass, Carol Shiner Wilson, J. Lawrence Mitchell, and John O'Brien kindly offered examples of authorial practices they found and often let me raid their libraries.

The Internet permitted me to receive assistance from invisible readers: Isobel Grundy, Jeslyn Medoff, Kathryn King, Gary E. Walker, Anna Kirkwood, George Justice, Patrick Leary, Bernard Hibbits, and Priscilla Murphy all helpfully responded to requests for information on the Women Writers Project, SHARP, and 18th Century Lists. Most recently, I have benefited from my acquaintance with the newly created Perdita Project, headed by Elizabeth Clarke, whose goal is to create an electronic database of early modern women's manuscript texts.

Part of the research for this volume was conducted while I was supported by a Creative and Scholarly Enhancement Research Award, Texas A&M

University; my thanks to Professor Robert Kennedy for his administration of this program. I likewise benefited from a Summer Research Fellowship given by the Interdisciplinary Group for Historical Literary Studies at Texas A&M and, as always, from the intellectual community that group offered.

I furthermore appreciate the permission of the *South Central Review* to reprint Chapter 6, which first appeared in that journal in 1994. My thanks, too, to Kari Kraus and Victoria Burke for permission to cite their unpublished thesis and dissertation. I am also grateful to the following individuals and libraries for permission to quote from their manuscript collections: the President and Fellows of Magdalen College, Oxford, the Royal Society of London, the Huntington Library, the British Library, and the Bodleian Library, Oxford.

SOCIAL AUTHORSHIP
and the
ADVENT OF PRINT

Introduction

The Changing Culture of Authorship and the History of the Book

For the historian, the book is always a perplexing object. Wrapped in its title as if in a timeless definition, the book is forever enclosed, and yet it never ceases to take on successive meanings.   FRANÇOIS FURET, *In the Workshop of History*

The wish to see one's work in print (fixed forever with one's name in card files and anthologies) is different from the desire to pen lines that could never get fixed in a permanent form, might be lost forever, altered by copying. . . . Until it became possible to distinguish between composing a poem and reciting one, or writing a book and copying one; until books could be classified by something other than incipits; how could the modern game of books and authors be played?   ELIZABETH EISENSTEIN, *The Printing Press as an Agent of Change*

This collection of essays looks at the material conditions of being an author at the turn of the seventeenth century and at literary culture immediately preceding the institution of copyright law in Britain. I am interested in considering both the book as an artifact, an object of material production and subject with all its problems to historical analysis, and, more speculatively, how the "game" of authorship was played in the period in which print was becoming the dominant, conventional mode of transmitting what we consider literary and academic writings but also during which manuscript circulation was still a viable and competitive technology. The following investigations are also shaped by present-day concerns with changing notions of the authorship and of the book in an age of competing technologies, in our times, printed versus electronic texts. With our own technological shifts have come an increasing awareness on the part of literary historians of the effect of the technologies of the material production of texts on the reception and subsequent analysis of their authors.

To pursue these inquiries I examine the ways in which traditional literary history overlaps with, but has remained largely separate from, the emerging field of "the history of the book" and the ways in which our perceptions of what "being an author" have been directed by an interest in evolving rather than residual technology. At the heart of this disjuncture between traditional literary history, bibliography, histories of the book, and new histories of reading and writing lies a series of related issues. The first is how one defines the book as an object of historical analysis. The second is more specifically a lack of artifactual, documentary information about how the game of authorship was indeed "played" by its participants, including those who were not living in the locations where we have traditionally placed literary culture. In existing studies of the book, scholars have taken little account of a quite basic question: Who was writing and who was reading as opposed to who was printing and who was purchasing? If one was a young poet living in the Welsh Marches in the 1690s, or a woman living almost anywhere outside London, what did it mean to be an "author"? Who read your writings? Whom did you read? If you wished to publish your literary or academic texts, how did you proceed? We have created theories to explain the silence or absence of women writers and those not living in London, Edinburgh, or the university cities, but we have not actively investigated the nature of literary life in the provinces; we have not yet integrated social, manuscript authorship practices with the history of commercial print authorship.

For Furet, one of the founders of the French *annales* school of historiography, the study of the printed book "crystallizes all the difficulties of the historian's craft: the passage from the individual to the collective, the relation between the intellectual and the social, time's judgments on time, the measure of innovation and inertia."[1] For the Anglo-American literary critic, the printed book occupies the dual function of being both the object of aesthetic study and, simultaneously, the marker of a successful intellectual career, a criterion of authorship increasingly coming under scrutiny because of the arrival of competing electronic technologies. These issues and concerns raised about electronic publication suggest some questions we may use to interrogate our understanding of previous shifts in literary technology.

Our own awareness as academic authors of the changing technologies of textual production comes at a time when the histories of the book and of reading have been rapidly developing.[2] Led by an interest in recovering the history of the reader usually forgotten by formalist criticism, a new group of historians and literary critics in France have been exploring *"l'histoire du livre à l'histoire de la lecture."*[3] As students of early modern British literature increasingly begin to turn attention to writing histories of authors and of reading, it is wise to keep in mind the problematic relationship of the reader, the critic, and the material processes of creating and distributing books that also characterizes our own historical moment. In recognizing and analyzing Furet's notions of "time's judgments on time" and Eisenstein's "games of books and authors" simultaneously with reconstructing the historical context of generations whose conditions and expectations of authorship are so different from the present's, we are well situated to see ways in which new questions arise and new models for literary history could be developed.[4]

The following pieces therefore consider how the expectations of previous historians have shaped the questions and perceptions we have of authorship in addition to offering a reconstruction of the material considerations of some representative authors involved in manuscript culture. Such a mixed approach may seem to some too close to history or historical sociology to be considered literary history in the classic sense;[5] nevertheless, I feel confident that such multidisciplinary approaches may result not only in the recovery of "perished" authors but also in a clarification in our sense of the literary past as being "the past" and how it is distinct from the present. These approaches may also provide an opportunity to rethink our current assumptions about who writes and who reads.

As part of my research, I have sought to understand the various processes by which historians of different generations both "lose" and "find" such individuals. This seemingly casual handling of past experiences is caused in part, I believe, by the very different notions of playing the game of authorship held by writers and readers in late-seventeenth-century Britain. It has been caused, too, in part by the impact of print technology on habits of reading and writing that traditionally have been studied separately from consideration of "literary" matters. As the following pieces explore, while attention has been given to the specific issue of gender and print technology, little has been allotted to the equally important and related issues concerning the geographic situation of the author or the nature of the anticipated audience and the influence of these factors on the author's choice of "publication" practices.

The author's choice of the means of transmission of his or her texts carries with it typically unexamined implications for the ways in which that author has been studied and transmitted by subsequent generations. When we come to look at social or provincial writers, we do so only through a previously determined set of expectations; the analysis we do of them tends to isolate and fragment the literary culture in which they participate. For an author working in the post–English Civil War period, publication traditionally has secured the individual his (although seldom her) place in recorded literary history. Making use of new studies on the history of the material book, literacy, and the development of copyright law in combination with the older archival research on printers, publishers, booksellers, and authors creates new possibilities for recovering writers and readers who existed on the margins of the commercial literary domain, a group whose participation in literary culture at large may be less marginal than their geographic situation suggests.

With the advent of electronic publication, we, too, as academic authors, are now confronted with new sets of questions concerning the nature of a "book" and its significance for how we write and read. The availability of a new form of "publication" technology not only destabilizes the boundaries of what we expect as an indicator of professional achievement but also highlights the writer's and reader's shifting expectations about different modes of text production.[6] Spirited debates occur over the setting up of "electronic preprint" archives, desiring to turn the Internet into a means of "author empowerment," declaring that "not only can scientific articles be published over the Internet 'unbelievably efficiently,' but they can be offered virtually free to all comers."[7] This very accessibility to technology, however, creates concerns: opponents to publishing academic works on the Net typically raise the issue of the lack of peer review before "publication," which, it is held, will weaken the intellectual standards of the discipline and flood the reader with a torrent of unreliable texts. If anyone sitting in her or his home can publish on the Net, can the resulting product be any good?

When the possibility of the electronic dissemination of text is added to a definition of authorship, the practical questions of how to evaluate it multiply dramatically. For academics, this typically arises during tenure review. Does creating software for composition classes "weigh" as much as writing an article for a refereed journal, or is it like a commercial textbook? Do pieces published in electronic journals or as part of electronic chat groups "count"? What about coauthored or collaborative pieces, which the electronic format makes so much more appealing and viable? Is a hypertext edition the equivalent of producing a diplomatic text or a variorum edition? Or, is it not an intellectual exercise but instead a technical one? Every year, university departments in the humanities grapple with such pragmatic questions, evolving answers as technology poses new challenges to our expectations of what an academic author is.[8]

Yes, the new "author" is faced with the necessity of acquiring new skills in order to take advantage of a medium of authorship. Electronic publishing, however, does not require endless delays in paper texts being read, set in type, copyedited, printed, bound, and shipped to market. The Internet offers a relatively free venue for those who possess the material means of accessing the technology and also opens a possibility of a worldwide readership almost as quickly as the words appear on the author's screen. It creates a space for authorship without the intervening presence of editor, bookseller, printer, or advertising agent. It is a mode of authorship in which the writer's gender and geographic location are significant primarily in terms of his or her access to technology. Finally, it offers a mode of authorship in which the author and reader can freely interact, with the possibility of creating a text that is an ongoing process of exchange rather than a commercial transaction.

Because we as academics are actively participating in this period of technological transition, confronting the possibilities as well as the limits of electronic publishing, we are ideally situated to examine our expectations and definitions of authorship as practiced in the past. Such an examination may also permit us to reconsider the ways in which earlier generations of writers—who experienced quite different material conditions for composition, distribution, and recompense for their literary works—confronted and adapted to the new print technologies associated with writing and marketing literature. Our own questions concerning how we arrive at our evaluations of authorship and how competing technologies affect both writers and readers place us in a good position to consider how earlier generations of print readers and print historians have treated the authors who lived and worked in the period immediately before the development of British copyright law and who were involved in the shift from scribal, manuscript texts and coterie readers to printed texts and a commercial readership.

As we all also know, for our literary culture, simply appearing in print does not absolutely prevent the author from perishing professionally. In our current situation, for example, prime importance is placed on the writing and publication of "the book," as a mark of professional success in the humanities. Not only by most tenure guidelines should there be a *published* monograph (not merely a completed or submitted manuscript, or at some institutions not even a manuscript accepted for publication), but it should be a single-author work and should be printed by a specific group of presses—university presses are broken into more or less desirable ranks and tiers, and typically one must make an argument for commercial presses as being suitable for tenure. The circumstances of a book's material production, its venue, and its level of commercial inflection affect its reception by the tenure committee and subsequently its author's standing in the professional academic literary community.

Likewise, as I have argued in earlier studies, traditional literary histories have also operated with a "tier" system of publication priorities. As I discuss in Chapter 1, traditional evocations of the literary history of the early modern period in Britain—for the purposes of this study concentrating on the 1650s through the early eighteenth century—are characterized by their use of print standards to reconstruct the culture of reading and writing. For the academic historian, the book as printed object has always carried a particular importance in delineating an author's activities and career as a writer. In addition to the single, concrete object, however, as I discuss in Chapter 6, the creation of a classic text from the early modern period has as much to do with who published the original as with the literary merit of the book's content. As I suggest in following essays, the time has come to consider alternative standards of evaluation and alternative modes of analysis not just to attempt to reconstruct the publication pattern and the sales of a text, or conversely, the mind-set of the individual author, but also to try to recover a sense of the literary environment in which writers wrote and readers read.

※

The history of the material culture of authorship—the material experience of writing and reading, the nature of the literary culture as well as the literary marketplace—is closely related to recent work on the history of the book itself, in which the material nature and conditions of the text rather than the individual author are the focus of analysis. As will be seen in the first three essays, my views about literary authorship during the Interregnum and Restoration periods in particular and authors' and readers' relationships with competing scribal and print technologies go against traditionally accepted beliefs in the beneficial, triumphant ascendance of print technology and commercial authorship during the English Civil War years and their supposed immediate dominance of the intellectual and literary culture during the Restoration and early eighteenth century. From Francis Bacon onwards—he advised that we study print along with the compass and gunpowder, "For these three have changed the appearance of the world"—the term "revolution" has been formulaically joined to discussions of print technology. Correspondingly, histories of print and of bookselling have framed their narratives as histories of a type of civil strife, with the new (young, democratic) technology overthrowing the established (old, aristocratic) one to usher in a new, better world. A representative sample of this underlying metaphorical construction of print can be seen in Christopher Small's study *The Printed Word: An Instrument of Popularity* (1982), which makes a direct link between the nature of the new technology and the English Civil War itself.

> Print as the means of spreading ideas among ordinary people assumed at this time a role so important, so indispensable, and so consciously used, that it became inextricably connected with the ideas themselves, and we find the right to print beginning to be claimed as a fundamental liberty, no less than those others which men were putting forward by its aid. Freedom of speech and freedom to print were formulated if not quite for the first time, with an unprecedented breadth of application, and the two went together, so much so that the difference between them (legal and other) were commonly ignored, and men demanded them as though the first naturally included the second.[9]

Small concludes that in England, in particular, "printing and political freedom were very closely linked; the unrestricted use of print was firmly associated with 'democracy'" (35).

As seen in this example, the English Civil War has tended to occupy a central and organizing position in histories of both British printing and bookselling. In traditional literary histories, it has also served as a watershed for authors and readers. Small believes that the printed word first came into its own as a genuinely popular medium during the war years. Recent studies such as Nigel Smith's work on the pamphlet press during the English Civil War and Margaret Spufford's classic exploration of the scope of seventeenth-century chapbooks have opened up a fascinating new world of the penny press, pamphlets, and popular literature and its readers and, in the process of doing so, have created a new and more sophisticated sense of literacy standards.[10] On the other hand, through such representations of the metaphorical ties of print and the English Civil War, in studies of the popular press in combination with more traditional literary histories focused on the major figures of the period, we have also perhaps received the impression of a world in which the printed text was the norm.

This positioning of the printed text as the norm for readers and writers after 1660 also spills over into other historical disciplines without much questioning. For example, in analyzing the quantitative evidence of scientific and agricultural progress between 1660 and 1780, those interested in "scientometrics" have attempted to the measure of the level of diffusion of ideas concerning agricultural improvement. The markers traditionally used to measure diffusion are the level of patenting (which is usually discussed in terms of its susceptibility to political and fiscal pressures) and the presence of publications, but in contrast to the variables acknowledged in studying patents, no mention is made of alternative methods of transmitting written information or the extent to which publication is a reliable indicator of practical change.[11]

This positioning of the 1640s and 1650s as the birth of a modern cultural era because of the "rise" of print and commercial authorship is continued in accounts of the 1670s through the early 1700s. The era after the war marks the stage in which the development of copyright law and the rise of the professional author are taken to be the significant transition point in literary history.[12] This characterization of late-seventeenth- and early-eighteenth-century literary culture as dominated by the new concerns raised by print is a basic premise in many literary histories of the period. Julie Stone Peters' study of Congreve and print culture, for example, bases her astute analysis on the unexamined premise that in the latter part of the seventeenth century, "writing and literacy become strongly identified with print, and the

Restoration had a sense of a world overflowing with the productions of the press."[13] While I agree with Alvin Kernan's position in his important study of Samuel Johnson and print that print technology forces "the writer, the scholar, and the teacher—the standard literary roles—to redefine themselves . . . [and] transform[s] the literary audience," as will be seen in the following essays, I must part company at his conclusion that during the early eighteenth century, "print . . . made literature objectively real for the first time."[14] Kernan goes on to characterize manuscript texts as "polite or courtly letters—primarily oral, aristocratic, amateur, authoritarian, court-centered," and as being swept away by the "new print-based, market-centered, democratic literary system" (4).

In these examples we can see clearly the continuation of the construction of print technology as a metaphor for the "new" and how it is associated with "modern" in a positive sense, and how it is simultaneously linked to "professional" authorship and "advanced" market economies. By implication—or as above, by direct statement—manuscript authorship and its readership have thus been relegated to the outdated, the primitive, and the "amateur." Obviously, one can understand the enthusiasm of historians of print for tracing the improvements and expansion of this technology, but as I discuss in the first two pieces, such constructions precede a description and analysis of the varied nature of the technology they were replacing.

Elizabeth Eisenstein lays out the seeming gap between the study of print and that of manuscript texts in *The Printing Press as an Agent of Change* by pointing to the intangible but real differences in the nature of authorship involved in the two practices.

> The wish to see one's work in print (fixed forever with one's name in card files and anthologies) is different from the desire to pen lines that could never get fixed in a permanent form, might be lost forever, altered by copying, or—if truly memorable—be carried by oral transmission and assigned ultimately to "anon." Until it became possible to distinguish between composing a poem and reciting one, or writing a book and copying one; until books could be classified by something other than incipits; how could the modern game of books and authors be played?[15]

Manuscript literary culture is thus positioned as the puzzle, the obstacle in a sense to progress and to the modernization of authorship and its democratic literary nature. Eisenstein does leave us with this study's starting point: How *was* the "game" of authorship played before copyright, when scribal copy still competed for its role in the literary culture?

When one turns to recent histories of reading, one encounters a similar problem in searching for information about manuscript readers. While those working on medieval materials are comfortable with discussing the nature of manuscript readership, what interests critics working during and after the Renaissance is the way in which print technology affected who read and how. Evelyn B. Tribble's ingenious study, for example, traces the history of relationship between author, reader, and authorities by looking at readers' additions to the margins of the printed text, but her concern is with printed, not script, texts.[16] In a similar fashion, John Kerrigan's thoughtful critique of Jerome McGann's theories as applied to Renaissance rather than romantic texts focuses on the ways in which Renaissance print technology engaged its original readers. "Renaissance books have the traits which they possess not simply because of authorial or print-shop peculiarities," Kerrigan posits, "but because they have certain designs upon, or hopes of interacting with readers."[17] The editors of the volume in which Kerrigan's essay appears, *The Practice and Representation of Reading in England,* observe that "evidence for popular reading in the early seventeenth century is slight, largely dependent on the survival of printed texts and contemporary descriptions of their reception" (17–18). Clearly, the history of reading, utilizing a wide range of analyses of material culture, from bibliographical to poststructuralist readings of the page, is an exciting new addition to literary history. As typified in *The Practice and Representation of Reading in England* it offers new ways of looking at familiar authors and texts exploring print culture, but, for those interested in manuscript readers after Chaucer, little guidance is given.[18]

In general, studies such as the ones cited above as well as more traditional literary histories (including Virginia Woolf's account of early modern women writers or institutional anthologies produced by commercial publishers such as Norton) treat the manuscript text as an aristocratic, anachronistic anomaly in the narrative history of authorship and do not distinguish the readership of script from print.[19] Authors embracing the older technology are often represented as refusing to embrace the modern age, "to play the game" of modern authorship. Small, for example, notes, "It is amusing and instructive to be told how the aristocratic connoisseur of books looked down his nose, to begin with, on the crude products of artificial writing"

(35). In Marjorie Plant's invaluable study of the English book trade, the argument also relies on the connections of class and technology in the following description of a scribal text:

> The employment of the scrivener in copying books survived longer in England than in any other country, owing to the exigencies of fashion. In the Elizabethan period it was considered beneath the dignity of a gentleman to have any dealings with a publisher; it was therefore customary for courtiers to circulate manuscript copies of their works among their friends.[20]

In this example, students interested in studying manuscript texts in the late seventeenth century find themselves seemingly facing a dead end—scribal copy is represented as being an outdated, frivolous aristocratic fashion in the sixteenth century, long before the English Civil War and its supposed liberating effects on authors. For a final example of this position, we see in Mark Rose's history of copyright in England how he divides authors into two modes, with print being associated with "modern" authorship; Rose places authors whose works remained in manuscript outside the "advanced marketplace society of the late seventeenth and early eighteenth centuries," and these authors thus stayed instead within a system of patronage, a "complex set of symbolic and material transactions" (*Authors and Owners*, 16). It is important to note that in both of Rose's categories, the author is characterized as a person writing for material gain, whether cash or influence with more powerful readers.

As has been suggested in these examples and will be explored further in the following chapters, the history of authorship in late-seventeenth-century Britain and in particular the history of manuscript transmission of literary texts have been delineated and controlled by a set of metaphors based on assumptions about class and technology and on gender and technology. In this story about authorship, print publication takes on the heroic role of the revolutionary force, usually represented by male writers eager to seize new opportunities, while manuscript culture has the role of the villain—the elitist, snobby aristocrat, very often a woman, clinging to long-outmoded forms in a futile attempt to retain control and power. In contrast to these existing interpretations of the heroic, democratizing impact of print technology in the seventeenth century, I explore in the following set of essays the cultural world of the script author and the "hidden" female participation in it both as author and as reader.

I argue that even after 1710 and the institution of the Act of Queen Anne, script was still a competitive, if not the dominant, mode of transmitting and reading what we term "literary" and "academic" materials. Rather than being a nostalgic clinging to an outdated technology representing a fading aristocratic possession of the world of letters, the older practice of circulating scribal texts was instead a choice. This authorial act was characteristic of very different physical conditions of writing and reading as well as a different self-definition of authorship, and indeed manuscript culture permitted and encouraged participation in literary life of groups of people whom print technology effectively isolated and alienated.

As Mark Rose noted, the history of the modern author is marked by the establishment of copyright or the establishment of the concept of "literary property," where the printed text is owned by an author. As he also notes, however, the battle to establish copyright was carried on not by the authors themselves but by the booksellers (3–5). His observation underlines my sense that we still need a history of authorship that is concerned with the author's, not the printer's or bookseller's, experience of writing in the material conditions of the times. Furthermore, we still need histories of authors and readers—often women—who resided away from the centers of publishing and the technology of "modern" authors. In short, we still need studies that are not focused on the "advanced" or modern concept of authorship during this period of transition but instead on all the varied aspects of the material culture of literature, especially as they are affected by geographic location and by the gender of the writer or the reader. Finally, we still need studies of the history of authorship and readers during the late seventeenth and early eighteenth centuries that do not consider the relationship between the writer and his or her reader as being governed only by commercial exchange or professional advancement.

To take such a position is not to claim that polemical and commercial literature did not flourish in this particular period. All one must do is to peruse the *Short Title Catalogue* to know that the primary intent behind works such as *The Whore's Rhetoric* (1681) or *Henry Marten's Familiar Letters to His Lady of Delight* (1662) was to earn money through providing entertainment to as many paying customers as possible. The remainder of the short pamphlets appearing in this period were largely statements in support of a political or religious cause.

It is important, however, when speaking of a literary culture that was supposedly becoming dominated by print technology and "modern" consciousness about authorship, to see what type of author actually did get into print during this period. Of the 3,550-plus printed texts so far counted that appeared between 1666 and 1680, studies by Plant, Friedman, and Smith, for example, show us that more than half of them were single sermons or tracts (which should alert us from the start that genre or subject matter will be as significant a factor as "class" in determining who embraced the new technology and who held fast to the old).[21] Despite the premise used by literary historians such as Peters and Kernan that print was dominant in the reading culture, it should be noted that, of these more than three thousand titles, pamphlets and small books made up the vast majority of the sum after the sermons; Friedman has calculated that the broadside ballads "were the most popular printed format in England" (7). Thus, while later generations have seen in these three thousand–plus titles a "flood" of print technology sweeping away the older modes of literary circulation or diffusion, the material pieces themselves—what was available to be read in print as opposed to in manuscript form—do not show a rush of "literary" authors as such to the new technology. Although studies have created a sense of the sudden burgeoning of the printers' and booksellers' business after the Civil War, it is instructive to explore, as we shall in Chapters 3 and 4, how very few presses operated in late-seventeenth-century Britain and under what conditions.

As we proceed to consider the different facets of literary life in late-seventeenth-century Britain, the need for such detailed, specific analysis of who published and how much was printed becomes obvious. In addition to the focus on the purely economic aspects of authorship, however, traditional literary histories have tended to behave as if the definition and classifications of authorship that govern their own activities existed for earlier periods. While it is acknowledged that the machines of production may be powered differently, it is also assumed, if not directly stated, that the human emotional or psychological dimension of authorship is a universal, transcendent phenomenon. Such a position, we need to notice, does suggest that the act of authorship is separate from the medium in which the writer

worked, and indeed, for the generations trained as New Critics and formal-
ists, the mechanical aspect of the production of texts was deemed largely
irrelevant.[22]

This position of studying the author's text separately from his or her historical and material moment obviously has been strongly challenged by
newer modes of historicisms as well as by those interested in the author as a
function and the text as a cultural product. As Jonathan Rose notes, the "old
book history" was concerned with "chronicling publishing firms, recovering
library catalogues and borrowing records, calculating levels of literacy, and
generally trying to determine which books a given body of readers owned or
read."[23] In the "new" book history, "the act of reading has emerged as a subject of concern; that is, not merely the what but the how, or process of reading. We have come to realize that modes of using and understanding print
changed over time."[24] In this definition, the "new" history of the book is
concerned with changing responses to print—this study is concerned with
the continued response to script by both writers and readers as part of the
overall project of understanding not only the "what" but the "how" of being
an author and being a reader in early modern Britain.

G. Thomas Tanselle likewise encourages us to adopt the pursuit of
"material culture," the study of physical objects or human artifacts as the
"direct products of mental activity," as the "prime activity of all who are
concerned with the past. . . . There cannot be a history of ideas without a
history of objects."[25] In a sense, the essays in this volume are largely concerned with a type of physical artifact that falls outside Tanselle's call for a
new type of literary history in that they are primarily concerned with the
handwritten rather than the printed text; Tanselle, who acknowledges the
"importance of handwriting as a means of transmitting visible language,"
nevertheless believes that "for a significant part of the past five centuries,
printed books were the primary means for disseminating verbal works, both
new and old," and that the "connections between texts and the physical
means of their production [apply] equally to manuscripts" (271 n. 6).

My starting position is that since we have no encompassing description
of the material culture of manuscript authorship in the late seventeenth and
early eighteenth centuries as opposed to studies of a few isolated individuals, we cannot automatically assume that the process of the creation, distribution, and consumption of manuscript texts parallels that of print ones.
Tanselle's design is to underline the crucial importance to the writing of his-

tory in considering the ways in which "texts are affected in the printing process. This simple, but profoundly important, point has remained outside the ken of most readers (even highly perceptive ones) over the centuries" (274). This study is concerned with examining those texts that were manuscripts not intended for print and with the culture of reading and writing that generated them. By looking at the ways in which manuscript text entered into the print process in the transitional period punctuated by the lapse of the Licensing Act in 1695 and the 1709 Act of Queen Anne, one can learn much about the history not only of publication but also of social writing and manuscript transmission.

It is important to notice at the start in these new historicisms, too, that theoretical structures devised to analyze the historical conditions governing authorship and to determine the features considered to be most important in shaping authorship—the development of a concept of the text as a "product" or the possession of a single individual along with the legal definitions of authorship and modes of attribution—are often based on Continental models, not British ones. While Foucault posits that "there are . . . transhistorical constants in the rules that govern the construction of an author," the time frame of the development of such a concept of the author is dependent on the external legal structures governing discourse; thus, a European model does not necessarily mesh well with the conditions of authorship in Britain.[26] Foucault's model is based on the premise that it was not until "a system of ownership and strict copyright rules were established (toward the end of the eighteenth and the beginning of the nineteenth century) that the transgressive properties always intrinsic to the act of writing became the forceful imperative of literature."

In contrast to Foucault's chronology, however, Rose claims in his study of British copyright that "politically, socially, and economically, eighteenth-century Britain was the most advanced country in Europe, and it was there that the world's first copyright statute was enacted in 1710" (*Authors and Owners,* 4). In short, the generalizations concerning what features constitute authorship on which Foucault's model is established ahistorically posit that only printed texts are markers of being an author; this is further complicated when transferred to Britain, where historians of print and its legal institutions clearly believe that the institutions of print were different from those in the rest of Europe. The changing legal conditions relating to authorship in Britain suggest that the period of the 1650s through the 1720s is an ideal one for evaluating the usefulness of such "what is an author?" models of history for a British experience, since manuscript and print cultures existed simultaneously (and, I argue, competitively and companionably) even after what was arguably the first copyright law was enacted in 1710.[27]

As we shall see, the historical development of text as property in Britain had a different trajectory than that on the Continent, which may affect not only our application of Foucault's model of the author but also that theorized by the *historie du livre* for France. Such Continental theories of authorship, however, are nevertheless of immense value in suggesting possible questions, issues, and practices that might be applied to this particular moment in British authorship. Henri-Jean Martin, in his grand and sweeping *History and Power of Writing,* is interested in the transition from oral culture to *printed.* In his discussion of the seventeenth and eighteenth centuries in Europe, manuscripts themselves vanish except as they are models for early printers to mimic and later as they represent the raw materials to be worked into the final printed product and marketed: "Around 1500 printing conquered Europe. It was to reign supreme over the continent for four centuries and move out to conquer the world."[28] In such histories, the manuscript text exists only as raw material for the presses.

Roger Chartier, likewise, in *The Order of Books,* makes it clear that it is the print text and "the effects of the penetration of printed written matter on the culture of the greater number" that is his concern (22–23). Chartier critiques the early efforts of Lucien Febvre and Henri-Jean Martin, noting that "in the tradition of the social history of print as it has developed in France books have readers but they do not have authors—or, more precisely, authors do not enter into that history's domain of competence: they are wholly the province of literary history and its time-honored genres—biography, the study of a school or current, or the description of an intellectual milieu" (27). His own study of reading, however, follows the traditional definition of authorship based on Richelet's *Dictionaire Français* (1680) and Furetière's *Dictionnnarie universel* (1690), where the "term 'author' is not to be applied to anyone who writes a work; the term distinguishes among all 'writers' only those who have cared to have their compositions published. Writing was not enough if one wanted to *s'ériger en auteur;* one's work also had to circulate in public by means of print" (41). Such views of the manuscript text, although they represent different aspects of the work done in *his-*

toire du livre, are similar to the English studies in their dismissal or disregard of the supposedly anachronistic practice of manuscript literary culture.

At the time this study was conducted, few critics of English literature of the Restoration and early modern period had worked on the phenomenon. Essential to understanding the literary culture of the Restoration, Harold Love's study *Scribal Publication in Seventeenth-Century England* devotes a complete monograph to exploring the ways in which scribal copies substituted for print texts in particular circumstances. His primary interest is in those texts that were "the creation of professional scribes, whose work was distributed through organized markets," and his case studies are of professionally assembled miscellanies, scribal proceedings from Parliament, and the scribal reproduction of music, with much less consideration of less "organized" manuscript practices.[29] In short, one of Love's main interests is the way in which an older form of publication technology mimicked the new technology's physical appearance, if not its nature. Love's study is less interested in the dynamics of coterie or manuscript authorship than in the ways in which an older authorial practice is adapted to the uses of the new. Although its subject matter is manuscript material, as I argue in the first essay, nevertheless, the study is about commercial print practices.

What all of these theoretical models of authorship in the past do, in spite of their differences, is to erase the notion of manuscript authorship that did not have as its primary aim a commercial readership and, likewise, any sense of a culture of reading and writing in which it was engaged. Instead, the notion of author found in these disparate studies tends to dismiss noncommercial texts as "aristocratic," "amateur," and "vulnerable." As my opening example concerning tenure suggests, our notions of what constitutes authorship and how we evaluate a text in this situation are indeed linked to venue and to textual production. For the purposes of this introduction, I would like to conclude by discussing some contemporary assumptions about being an author in the framework of the latter part of the seventeenth century, a period in which I believe script and print in Britain were still actively competing technologies. In particular, I want to look at our current concern with "publishing and perishing" and with notions such as the "death of the author" in the context of the experience of authorship.

It is obvious, of course, that the simple act of publishing did not prevent an author from perishing in the pages of traditional literary histories. Traditional attempts to map histories of literary culture, such as Taine's and Dobrée's, which had as their goal the understanding of the "spirit of the age" through analyzing key texts, necessarily omitted the vast majority of published authors from their pages.[30] Even more restricted general surveys of literary life, such as Sutherland's and Wedgewood's reviews of particular centuries, do not dwell on many literary figures who are the object of study in the present day.[31] Virginia Woolf believed that women did not write before Aphra Behn, except for a few isolated eccentrics; we know now that this simply is not true. When one consults the index of the Oxford History of English Literature series, one will search in vain for writers who wrote in English but who lived in Scotland, Ireland, or Wales, unless one knows in advance who they are. Why did such early modern authors—whether women or Scots or the Welsh—not survive in the pages of literary history?

To begin with, few literary histories or histories of authorship have taken into account that even the term I have been using—*British*—is an anachronistic label imposing order and uniformity on a cultural geography that did not even legally exist until the Act of Union in 1707. While accounts of authors' lives conventionally include accounts of male writers' years spent at Oxford or Cambridge, few literary histories have paid much attention to the practical impact on an author of being born and raised in a Hampshire village or in Dumferline. Nor have we given much thought to the implications for the modes of reading and writing if the individual resided in Coventry, Exeter, or Bath, or the significance of having relatives who lived in London. Our literary histories typically have not looked at how being published in Edinburgh in the 1680s might be different from being published in London during the same time period. In the same way that we have theorized authorship before having a good descriptive model of scribal practices, we have tended to analyze early modern authorship as if region made little difference. In the same way that we have accepted the view that, by the Restoration period, all authors wrote for print publication, we have tended to behave as if geography were irrelevant and as if, even before the passage of the Act of Union, there was a unified, uniform culture of literary and academic authorship. As we shall see in Chapters 4 and 5, however, where one was living and where one's relatives were located often constituted a decisive in the writer's decisions about publishing and manuscript circulation.

As Roland Barthes long ago observed, modern criticism is obsessed with the figure of the author as the source of explanation, and we who work in literary history have concentrated on reimaging that individual's desires as an explanation for authorial choices to the extent of denying that that individual was part of a culture whose reading and writing practices are quite different from our own. Classical literary histories of the early modern period such as Taine's or Edmund Gosse's searched in the personality of a representative individual for the "spirit of the age," to recapture the mentality of an era. More recent historical studies of the period often see the author as an outsider, alien to the culture that produced him or her. The result of both of these notions of the author in the past is that we have had to come up with some quite extraordinary methods to erase—or rather to mask—the differences between past and present and that we are positively flummoxed by the writer who had no desire to see his or her work in print or to play our games of authorship.

New historians of the book and of the history of bibliography, such as Tanselle, Jerome McGann, D. F. McKenzie, Robert Darnton, and Roger Chartier, have asked us in various ways to attempt to recapture the notion of the text as a material object and a cultural product. For the early modern period, the notion of authorship needs to become less a lament for the "fate" of the author and more of a recovery of what Chartier terms "the networks of practices that organize the historically and socially differentiated modes of access to texts" (53). Chartier, writing on issues of literacy leading up to the French Revolution, reminds us that "authors do not write books. Rather they write texts which become objects copied, handwritten, etched, printed, and today computerized," a gap that he calls "the space in which meaning is constructed, [which] has too often been forgotten not only by classical literary history, which thinks of the work in itself as an abstract text for which the typographical forms are unimportant, but even by *Rezeptionstheorie*" (53). He concludes in his call for a new type of history of the book that "we must insist that there is no text outside the material structure in which it is given to be read or heard. Thus there is no comprehension of writing, whatever it may be, which does not depend in part upon the forms in which it comes to its reader" (53). The task of this study is in part to describe some of the differences in the ways in which texts came to readers in the late seventeenth century and the start of the eighteenth and in part to explore subsequent generations' perceptions of the material culture of authorship.

In our enthusiasm for the new technology of print and for tracing the "rise" or "emergence" of professional authorship, we have been distracted from considering the lived, material conditions of reading and writing during the late seventeenth and early eighteenth centuries in what would come to be called Great Britain. Although we may not claim an interest in the history of the book, assumptions about the historical conditions of authorship permeate our critical assumptions about individual texts and writers and have, in fact, caused a whole class of authors to perish in the pages of our literary studies, both manuscript authors and published ones.

However, it is not too late to recover these writers and the conditions under which they wrote and their readers received them. For ourselves, it will be interesting to see how the academy will respond as we face our own equivalent of the shift in publishing technologies. How will we modify our notions of authorship in the coming years, with the advent of virtual journals? How will we evaluate our colleagues' publications when we ourselves drown trying to surf the Net? Will creating a hypertext edition be considered a scholarly publication or technological witchcraft? Looking back at the script writers of the Restoration, we have to wonder, as we are pirated onto a discussion board on the Net, will we find a way to preserve and take pleasure in our archaic print texts, or will we perish as anachronisms? These questions now facing us are merely the rephrasing of the question raised in the late seventeenth century: What will it mean to be an author in the twenty-first century?

ONE

The Social Author

Manuscript Culture,
Writers, and Readers

I absolutely prohibit and discharge any of my Posterity from lending [this manuscript] or dispersing them abroad. They are to remain in the House of Pennicuik. Sir John Clerk, *Memoirs of the Life of Sir John Clerk of Penicuik*

The prime lesson one learns from studying these manuscripts in depth is that in [the early seventeenth century], from which so much remains unprinted, one never dares make too confident an assertion about poets, poems or poetry: a new manuscript may turn up tomorrow which radically alters the picture.

Mary Hobbs, "Early Seventeenth-Century Verse Miscellanies and Their Value for Textual Editors."

In her studies of manuscript miscellanies from the first part of the seventeenth century, Mary Hobbs declares that "the proper use of manuscript miscellanies is, in short, the way to a fuller, more accurate, study of early seventeenth-century poetry."[1] One of the first issues to consider when discussing later-seventeenth-century manuscript authorship in comparison with print publication practices in early modern England, Scotland, and Wales is the simple pragmatic matter of getting into print, and whether or not conditions of authorship had universally changed from that suggested by Hobbs' remarks. Was print a more desirable technology for writers, in particular literary authors, living in the latter part of the seventeenth century? At its most elemental level, assuming that the author desired to be in print (which, as we shall see in this essay, cannot automatically be assumed to be the case, even in the early eighteenth century),[2] the whole issue of the re-

21

lationship between writers and print technology in early modern Britain comes down to considering the following questions. Suppose an author, living in a small village in the 1650s or even as late as the 1690s, wrote a poem: What were his or her options to secure readers? What are the terms and models we have available to describe the experience of authorship in this period? How have the terms that have been used to narrate the process of authorship and progress of print shaped our perspectives on past experiences and our expectations about early modern literary culture?

Before tackling the pragmatics of print, we must gain a clearer sense of what manuscript authorship entailed, of what the expectations of both its authors and its readers were. At this stage, the latter part of the seventeenth and the first part of the eighteenth century still lack a clear description of the nature of manuscript literary activity, much less a theory of nonprint literary culture, of the sort that critics working with late medieval and Renaissance texts have been constructing.[3] In this study, I am not dealing with the phenomenon described by Harold Love as "scribal publication," whereby professional scribes reproduced the appearance of print texts, but instead I am concerned with that group of writers and readers who used script as an alternative or in addition to purchased printed texts.

Love's study, important as it is for understanding the texture of Restoration literary life, demonstrates one of the problems of discussing the culture of authorship during this period. Even though the subject of Love's study is manuscript texts, the focus of the analysis is largely in the context of print and its norms. For example, we see the privileging of print in his choice to analyze the social function of script texts as vehicles "by which ideologically charged texts could be distributed through the governing class, or various interest-groups within that class, without their coming to the knowledge of the governed" (177). In the same way, in Love's view, women writers chose scribal texts because "the stigma of print bore particularly hard on women writers" (i.e., they would have chosen print if they dared) (54). Love also believes that women's "literary writings circulated in this way were quantitatively of minor significance beside the texts by women writers dealing with the practical conduct of the household, the preparation of food and clothing and the treatment of illness. Personal collections on these subjects were regarded with great pride by their compilers" (58).

Unlike Love, I believe that we have little or no sense of the actual scale of women's literary participation in manuscript culture apart from a few celebrated examples. Until quite recently little effort has been made to catalogue and reconstruct patterns in women's manuscript texts to provide an inclusive overview of literary activities rather than isolated, individual authors.[4] Certainly, given our current state of knowledge, we have little or no sense of the pride (or lack thereof) felt by women authors who used manuscript circulation for literary materials in comparison to domestic ones.

This perception of the author's motive for choosing manuscript text over print—that it was for political reasons—is also the view of manuscript authorship in the Restoration espoused by Woudhuysen. Looking at the practice over the course of the seventeenth century, Woudhuysen, along with Marotti, sees the trajectory of the practice as follows: "By about 1640 scribal publication seems to have begun to decline. . . . [It] faltered in the 1640s and the 1650s, but gained new life with the Restoration, playing a leading role in the dissemination of satirical writings" (391). The point made by Love, and Woudhuysen, about writers using script to circumvent censorship is perfectly correct, but the implication behind the terms of analysis is that we seek to understand the manuscript text by analyzing it for what it is *not*, that is, it is "not print" because of the structures of power. The investigative starting point appears to be "why didn't this author use print?" rather than "what is this author attempting to do?"

As in earlier studies involving manuscripts from this period, such as David Vieth's *Attribution in Restoration Verse,* which attempts to bring editorial order to the chaotic world of Restoration coterie verse exchanges, the critical focus also tends to be on the *problems* manuscripts and coterie groups create for print editors; part 3 of Love's study is concerned with editing scribally published texts. Who wrote which lines? Which of the multiple manuscript copies is "authentic" and which of the multiple manuscript versions will best serve as the copy text for a print edition? All of these legitimate editorial questions divert our attention, however, from the manuscript culture that creates such confusion in its refusal to conform to the linear chronology of the modern print text: a rough draft leads to a final draft or copy text, which leads to print. Instead of seeking to describe the activities of the author and his or her manuscripts before they are forever fixed in print, current studies of manuscripts from the late seventeenth and early eighteenth centuries have instead focused on their relationship to print culture and how best to convert them to print volumes.

As part of this focus on the printed text, studies such as those by Vieth and Love, and even studies of specific individuals involved in manuscript circulation, are primarily interested in the links between a scribal text and a printed one. We see, for example, in Brice Harris's early study of Robert Julian—a professional scribe who collected and distributed manuscript lampoons and satires by Dorset, Buckingham, Rochester, and their friends—one of the first studies of the way in which manuscripts were exchanged at a central London location, in this case Will's Coffee House. For Harris, however, the point of the investigation is Julian's commercialization of these texts, a literary career that "forms an important, though lurid, chapter in the early annals of Grub Street, in the distribution of scatological literature, and in the bizarre attempts of the low and unliterary to make a living by their pens."[5] The manuscript texts themselves disappear except as they provide commercial materials for the professional scribe: "Julian's so furnish'd by these scribling Sparks / That he pays off old Scores and keeps two Clarkes" (304). Although Harris's study provides a fascinating glimpse into the economics of manuscript transcription and the legal penalties for libel, we easily lose sight of the authors who provided the original material, the circumstances of its composition, and the circulation of the different versions in addition to Julian's commercial copies. We do not see any aspects of the world of the manuscript author who did not care to see his or her works in print or derive an income from them or, indeed, of the manuscript author's readers.

What has been left out of existing literary histories of the Restoration and early eighteenth century is a sense of authorship and readers that existed independently from the conventions and the restrictions of print and commercial texts. While we are quite content to accept the fact that the quality of John Donne's secular verse or Sir Philip Sidney's was not compromised because they were "amateur" authors writing for a coterie readership, when we study the latter part of the seventeenth century, we seem to impose Samuel Johnson's later-eighteenth-century pronouncement that only blockheads write for anything except money. There exists an imaginative gap in our thinking about writers during this transition period that led traditional histories into awkward and anachronistic configurations in the attempt to see them as prototype "modern" authors.

We see this configuration, for example, in traditional literary histories that tend to be organized around Dryden and Pope, two of the most successful commercial poets of their generations, or around the evolution of particular commercial literary genres. As we shall see in the next essay, the treatment of Pope in particular has focused on his commercial writings and his relationship with the paid hack writers of Grub Street. The standard literary histories extol the rise of the novel or commercial fiction during this period; likewise, the late seventeenth and early eighteenth centuries have assumed crucial importance in women's literary histories because of the ability of women to earn money through writing at this time. What has gotten lost in the focus on the professional author and the increasing popularity of commercial genres is any sense of a thriving amateur, social literary culture, such as we have seen explored for the early part of the seventeenth century by Mary Hobbs, Katherine Duncan-Jones, Arthur F. Marotti, and H. R. Woudhuysen. Although we have excellent studies of individual writers' manuscripts and their relationship to print production during this period, we have no sense of the patterns or practices of authorship as part of a group. We certainly have little sense of authorship for those writers residing outside London or the university cities, male or female. Unlike studies of the late sixteenth and early seventeenth centuries, traditional literary histories of the end of the seventeenth and the start of the eighteenth centuries have not yet developed a concept of an author's "public" that does not involve "publication" because of our fascination with the new possibilities for the commercial author and commodity-consuming reader.

To fill in some of the missing gaps in our perception of early modern manuscript authorship, we must begin with some very basic, practical questions. In simple terms of production, obviously, script texts could be produced at home, or even during travel, as long as the author was able to write or dictate to someone else. Several types of manuscript texts were produced, which have traditionally been classified as follows: single sheets, often showing folds where they were included as part of a letter; "common place books," which Vieth described as showing signs of being compiled over a period of time, with changes of ink, handwriting, and presentation, with heterogeneous contents; and "manuscript miscellanies," which he characterizes as "typically . . . a homogeneous collections [*sic*] of poems with perhaps some related prose pieces, likely to reflect careful selection and arrangement" and to have been copied over a short period of time.[6]

We can see all of these types of literary production in action in the mid-seventeenth-century collection called the Tixall Papers, which comprise the papers of the Aston family and include verses exchanged in letters, commonplace books, and several manuscript volumes of verse, compiled and arranged as volumes by members of the family. This collection, which was first edited by a family descendant in 1813, offers a partial presentation of long-past literary lives of men and women for whom reading, writing, and poetry were a passion and lifelong occupation.

The Aston and Thimelby families, along with their friends and relatives, lived relatively near one another in Lincolnshire and Staffordshire, linked by marriage and by their Catholic faith. As their nineteenth-century editor, Arthur Clifford, characterized the group,

> they were individuals of five distinct families, inhabiting a line of country in the very center of England, and none at a very great distance from the others. The Priory at St. Thomas [Constance Aston Fowler's home], is three miles from Tixall [the family home], which is five from Ballamore; and from that to Canwell is fifteen, which places are all in Staffordshire. From Canwell to Irnham [Gertrude Aston and Edward Thimelby's home] in Lincolnshire is about five and thirty miles.[7]

In the preface to *Tixall Poetry,* Clifford describes how, on a search for documents relating to Sir Ralph Sadler, the housekeeper at Tixall gave him a "great trunk" filled with papers, so many that he declares it took him ten days to sort through them. "It was a bumper, brimful, and overflowing," he recalls; "the enormous mass appeared to consist of papers of every sort, and size: the surface of which was most respectably defended, by a deep and venerable layer of literary dust" (viii).

After separating out what he considered to be the "literary" manuscripts, Clifford divided the materials into four groups, which forms the organization for his edition. The first section consists of the contents of a small quarto volume, with no cover but with "Her. Aston, 1658," on the outer leaf; the second section is from another small quarto, with no cover, whose first poem is "Mrs. Thimelby on the Death of her only child"; the third section of Clifford's volume is from a folio covered in parchment with "William Turner his booke 1662" inscribed on the outside and on the inside cover, "Catherin Gages booke," which Clifford decided were poems collected by Catherine Gage, Lady Aston; and the fourth section was composed of "a large quantity of loose scraps of paper, sheets, half-sheets, backs of letters, and the like, scribbled over with verses" (x).

The first three texts, the volumes Clifford lists as being by Herbert Aston, Gertrude Thimelby, and Catherine Gage, have not been recovered, but two other manuscript volumes apparently not described here by him have been found, one by Herbert Aston and the other by Constance Aston Fowler.[8] Between the two existing manuscript volumes and Clifford's nineteenth-century edition of the missing ones and the family correspondence, we have an extended example of the dynamics of manuscript authors and readers, in addition to information about how manuscript texts were produced, disseminated, and preserved in provincial areas.

The fourth section of *Tixall Poetry* was assembled from single-sheet texts, poems found on what Clifford describes as "backs of letters, or other scraps of paper" (xiii). In addition to poems by members of the Aston family—Sir Walter Aston, the head of the family; his third son, Herbert Aston, and his wife, Katherine Thimelby; his daughter Gertrude Aston Thimelby and her husband, Edward Thimelby; and his youngest child, Constance Aston Fowler—these "scraps" and letters record poems by Sir Richard Fanshawe, Sidney Godolphin, Edmund Waller, and John Dryden, which Clifford believed he was publishing for the first time (xiii). The "backs" of the letters not only served as scratch paper, as Clifford suggests, but clearly also were a means of transmission and of preservation of these single pieces. Clearly, too, the network of families not only exchanged their own verses in letters but also transmitted single copies of poems they read by others in manuscript form.

From such scraps of paper, several manuscript volumes were created. While her brother Herbert was serving with his father and with Sir Richard Fanshawe on a diplomatic mission in Spain, Constance Aston Fowler repeatedly wrote to him to send her some verses—"I want some good ones to put in my booke."[9] Constance Aston Fowler constructed her own private anthology, in which she mingled the poems of her family with ones by Ben Jonson, Henry King, and John Donne. It is important to note of this text that Fowler was not simply collecting edifying sayings or transcriptions from printed sources; rather, she was compiling her "book" through selecting "good" verses.[10] It is also of interest that in addition to her father's and her brother's poetic contributions, her sister Gertrude was a contributor, too, as was their friend Lady Dorothy Shirley; thus both men and women actively participated in this literary compilation.

At a later date, Herbert Aston's wife created another volume of her husband's verse. Concerning the construction of this volume, Herbert Aston wrote to his sister, "My Mrs. havinge nothinge else to doe this winter, hath made a slight collection of all my workes. Wherefore you must make an inquiry into all your papers, and if you find any of mine that beginn not as in this note, you must send them her by the first opportunity" (*Tixall Poetry,* xxii). He then includes a list of first lines of the poems his wife has already assembled. This example raises several interesting general points concerning manuscript authorship and readership. It is clear that manuscript verse existed in several formats: the initial one, obviously, transmitted through letter and forming part of a collection of loose papers or "scraps." The recipient of such script texts then frequently contributed a verse reply to the originating text, also on a loose sheet. It is the collection and arrangement of these loose materials that form the sequences in the later manuscript volume.

It is also interesting to note that Herbert Aston is not certain who has which of his texts. He requests his sister to go through her collected papers to see if she can find any poems with first lines not on the list he sends her, that is, poems of which he, the author, has no copies. Neither of these manuscript volumes was compiled with the intent to secure a printer; both were literary compilations, however, involving the talents and editorial skills of several individuals, using a range of manuscript texts in various forms compiled into a "book."

As we continue looking at examples from later on in the century, from the 1650s and 1660s, we find similar patterns for compilation volumes involving the labors either of family members or of nearby friends and community. Around 1651, Patrick Cary, the brother of the Cavalier hero Lucius Cary, created a small manuscript volume, which was eventually published as *Poems from a manuscript written in the Time of Oliver Cromwell* (1771) and then edited and reduced by Sir Walter Scott (who also encouraged Arthur Clifford's efforts) in 1819. His modern editor, Sister Veronica Delany, describes the creation of this manuscript volume of thirty poems as a compilation of social verses and religious meditations written while the young Patrick Cary was staying in a small Hampshire village, Wickham, with his sister, Lady Victoria Uvedale. The manuscript, in Cary's hand in a small notebook with a black leather cover, is divided into two sections; Delany notes that the pages containing songs show evidence of candle grease and wine stains, suggesting that the volume enjoyed an extended, if messy, literary life with generations of readers.

The first section is entitled "Triviall Ballades" and dated "1651 August 20th," with the declaration that the pieces are "writt here in obedience to Mrs Tomkins commands"; the second section, composed of religious and meditative verse, has on its opening page an inscription, "I will sing unto the LORD (Ps xiii.6)," with a coat of arms, a Tudor rose, and "Warneford, 1651."[11] This section also features an interesting set of carefully drawn emblems. The result is a volume demonstrating not only the range of the young author's literary tastes but also that of his readership:

> A varied flow of verse now came from the young man's pen. Political satires pelted Cromwell with high-spirited abuse; pastoral poems reflected the pleasures of the exile returned; love poetry paid debonair tribute to the ladies of the Uvedale circle, an appreciative audience, while witty occasional verse captured the atmosphere of Wickham and the friendly maisons of the neighborhood. (liii)

Cary's sister Victoria had been a maid of honor at the court of Henrietta Maria and had appeared in Walter Montagu's *The Shepheards Paradise* and Davenant's masques *The Temple of Love* and *Salamacida Spolia* in the mid- and late 1630s; in 1640, she married Sir William Uvedale, the treasurer of the Chamber (l–li). In the autumn of 1650, she welcomed her younger brother to Wickham after his "brief inglorious effort" at becoming a monk at the Benedictine cloister of St. Gregory's Priory, Douai (xlv–xlvii). Back in England, he clearly enjoyed a social community of like-minded Royalist readers, whom he portrayed along with their servants and children in his occasional verse.[12] The manuscript text he created not only was read by family members and friends residing nearby during the author's lifetime but eventually found its way into print a century after his death.

Nor was brother Patrick the only productive manuscript poet living at Wickham and inspired by Lady Victoria Uvedale. Some twenty years after Patrick Cary had written his collection there, Wickham was again the subject for an anonymous young man, who prepared a small collection of miscellaneous verse including "On the departure of the Lady Victoria Uvedall from Wickham 1672/3."[13] In this piece, the poet displays an extensive range of pathetic fallacies, where the natural surroundings decline with the departure of Lady Victoria Uvedale: "The sympathising Grove begins to fade / And all its beauties languish in a shade" (14). This poem is followed by "On the Grove at Wickham," which draws equally enthusiastic praise: "That fame impos'd on *Asia*, 'tis clear / In placing *Paradise* and *Eden* there, / The sacred relicks of that hallowed ground / Are no where but in Wickham to be found" (15).

Like the Tixall volumes prepared by Herbert Aston's wife, Katherine, this volume is also a compilation of a single author's works. Although it is attractively copied, with red-ruled margins and calligraphic flourishes at the ends of some of the poems, it appears to have been a "working" text rather than a final presentation copy. Some pieces show corrections while others show minor revisions.[14] Finally, some of the poems are completely marked out by large *X*s drawn over them; the poem on the author's depressing twentieth birthday is completely crossed over, while in other poems large sections are crossed through or heavily revised, as in his poem "The Chamber": "A Poem, To his timorous Countrymen complaining of his goeing Forth, forst him to keepe his Chamber after his recovery from the small pox" (20). The other poem completely crossed through concerns the poet's erotic dream of embracing a sleeping "Lorinda" (a female who had spurned him in other verses), whose bosom is temptingly exposed; this poem, however, opens with the disconcerting title "A dreame after Lorinda's death Poisoned by Thirsistes" and has the speaker "lying senseless on my bed / With wreathes of poppy coyl'd about my head" (60).

The author remains unidentified, although he offers some biographical clues in his verse, such as in one poem, "Upon his Birthday," in which he morosely announces that "I've been twice ten years extant, yet ther's none / Of them which I dare call, or vouch to be mine own" (33). The opening poem is "A Poem upon Blindness upon Bartholomew Price Esq Justice of the Peace," which, in addition to the two poems specifically addressing the Uvedal family, suggests that in addition to them (and the disdainful Lorinda) his verses had a local readership, and perhaps, like Cary, the volume was compiled at the request of his readers. As with Cary's decision to provide attractive emblems to illustrate his religious verse, this author also attempts to produce an attractive volume, with page numbers, marginal glosses, and calligraphic ornaments. On the whole, it leads one to the impression that Patrick Cary was certainly not alone in providing reading material for the families in the small community of Wickham or in his concern for creating his own "book," a manuscript compilation presented in an attractive volume. Neither gentleman gives any indication that he would like his volume to be published, and indeed, with the crossed-out sections of the volume, either the author or a later reader took pains to edit the two most personal pieces.

In another compilation volume, whose contents appear to have been composed between 1670 and 1690, we can see traces of this process whereby the provincial manuscript writer participated in a network of verse exchange, collected his own works, and finally compiled them into a volume in order to revise and edit it. John Chatwin matriculated at Emmanuel College, Cambridge, in 1682, apparently when he was only fifteen.[15] Chatwin, who also appears on the college books as "Chattins," was a contemporary of Matthew Prior's, who matriculated at St. John's College, Cambridge, the same year. Chatwin took a B.A. degree in 1685 and simply vanished from record. During his years at Cambridge, he produced quite a sizeable manuscript text of 280 pages of verse—complete with the title page "POEMS" and "A TABLE" of titles at the end of the volume; Chatwin left the last 80 pages blank, providing an opportunity for him to continue adding pieces.[16] From these references to particular events and people, it would appear that the pieces were composed when the poet was between sixteen and eighteen years of age: as Peter Giles, the only other commentator on his text, observed in 1897, the young poet had "no mean command of the rhyming couplet"; Giles added, "They are certainly as good as the effusions of Prior which can be traced to his undergraduate days, and Prior was considerably older when he entered College" (12, 22).

In this volume, believed by Giles to be a compilation volume arranged by the author rather than a chronological accumulation, there are poems referring to his time as a student at Emmanuel College, Cambridge ("To His Tutor, who punish'd Him for going to the Tavern"), some pieces that are strictly occasional, and some that commemorate national political and literary events. In addition to several poems on drinking and gout (the latter of which seems contrived for so young a poet), Chatwin preserved his poem "Made in the Tunns on a chamber-pot," referring to the "Three Tunns" inn on Castle Hill in Cambridge, which has the memorable opening "Hail serviceable Utensil!" (116). Other poems are concerned with more public social events and are addressed to friends who lived in Leicestershire, such as his godfather, William Cole, of Lutterworth, a justice of the peace; Chatwin wrote an elegy for Cole's first wife, Barbara, who died in the early 1680s, and an epithalamium for his second marriage to "Emm," the daughter of "Major Warner."[17] The Leicestershire origins of the volume are reinforced by other poems specifically concerned with a group of friends in the area: Chatwin laments the death of John Burroughs, rector of Stoneby, and includes a poem apparently composed in a friend's garden at the nearby village of Ashby Magna, "A Coppy of Verses made under the Yew Tree in the Honourable Mr. Finch's Orchard in Ashby Magna."[18]

In addition to his poems addressing family and local Leicestershire occasions, Chatwin was engaged by national events. The volume includes a poem on the anniversary of the death of Charles I, an elegy on the death of Charles II, and an epithalamium for the marriage of Princess Ann to Prince George of Denmark (1683). The last was Chatwin's only printed poem, appearing in the Cambridge University collection celebrating the marriage, *Hymenaus Cantabrigiensis,* published by John Hayes (1683), whose other contributors included William Fleetwood (future bishop of Ely), Charles Montagu (Trinity; afterwards earl of Halifax), and Matthew Prior. The poem on the death of Charles II is immediately followed in the manuscript volume by "Congratulations" to James II; he also wrote on the death of Buckingham, the duke of Ormond.

Chatwin's volume demonstrates his precocious skill in creating suitable verses not only for national occasions but also for events of note in the literary world. His poem "To the Pious Memory of Mrs. Ann Killigrew" demonstrates his enthusiasm both for her verse (which has him declaring, "Till she appear'd all Poetry lay dead / O'recharg'd and stifled in Its Infant-bed") and for Dryden's famous ode on the same occasion (149–50). He also writes on the death of Nell Gwynn, which suggests that even a young man raised in Leicester and in a strongly Puritan college in Cambridge could follow the royal scandals and London theater life. It is also worth noting that several of his poems are written in response to reading the poetry of others. In addition to the commemorative verse on Anne Killigrew's writings, Chatwin addresses one poem "To Astrea on her Poems" (50), which, given the reference to her praise of "Daphnis" (Creech), is clearly Aphra Behn.

It is not clear where or in what format Chatwin read Killigrew or Behn, but it is obvious from the contents of his volume that he was reading the manuscripts of other provincial poets. One such trace of Chatwin's reading found in his own manuscript verse is "On Mr. Wanley's most ingenious Poem the Witch of Endor" (115). Born in 1634 in Leicester, Nathaniel Wanley was the rector of Trinity Church in Coventry, having received his B.A. degree from Trinity College, Cambridge, in 1653 and his M.A. degree in

1657. In 1658, he was the minister at "Beeby" in Leicester; he married Ellen Bunton and had five children, one of whom was Humphrey Wanley, the future librarian for Harley. The poem praised by Chatwin, Wanley's "The Witch of Endor," exists in two manuscripts but was not printed until L. C. Martin "recovered" Wanley's verse in 1925.[19]

As with the anonymous young man in Hampshire, Chatwin (or a later reader, perhaps Rawlinson) also went through and x-ed through several poems, although, in the same manner as the previous volume, none of the strikeouts actually hinders the poem from being read. Like the strikethroughs marking the verse of the young man from Wickham, these poems tended to be his more erotic fantasies, such as "Lying on the Bed with Her," which concludes, "For the soft Raptures wee so well did prove, / I'de scorn, nay hate the petty joyes above" (48), and "The Fatigue," which opens, "When in my Armes charming Sylvia lay" (108). Chatwin published only one of the poems in this volume, although several are of very good style and polish. As this volume documents, he did circulate his manuscript verse, using it to respond to what he read and to comment on the significant public events of his day, both locally and nationally. Chatwin did save his texts, revise them, and finally, too, create a volume with a title page, whose contents he also continued to revise and edit, and quite clearly he and his readers considered his activity to be that of an "author" even though publication was never a feature.

A more elusive example can be found in the manuscript volume of John Hooper, a small vellum-bound paper volume whose contents appear to have been composed in the 1660s and perhaps early 1670s.[20] There are two possible candidates among Oxford students at this time for the poet, the most likely being John Hooper, the son of "Hieron" of Hatherly, Devon; he was admitted to Exeter College as a "Pauper Puer," matriculating 29 November 1667 at age nineteen.[21] It has a title page with "Verses" on it, and the author identifies himself at the end of a poem "uppon ye deathes of my Father and Brother who dyed in the yeare 1665." The title page also states the location to be "Devon," and in "To my Mother / Mis Mary Hooper" there is a notation in the side margin "A New Yeares Gift" (4r, 3r). On the verso side of this last poem is "Abraham Ivory" in a different hand. In addition to the poems about or to family members, the little volume contains meditations on Luke and Hosea and poems celebrating significant events in his friends' lives: "Epithilamium In celebration of the happie Nuptual of the much honord Master Hine and [?] endeared consort." Hooper also responds to the poetry of others, as seen in "A poem of Mr: Gosnalls who made it uppon the death of Miss Sarah Hawes." This volume appears to fall within the realm of Vieth's manuscript miscellanies, giving the appearance of having been a compilation of the author's works made during a comparatively short period of time; the titles of the poems suggest that Hooper had been a practicing poet in Devon, as well as a reader of the manuscript verse of others, for some years before the volume was assembled.

Another example of a family literary collection from the opposite end of the social scale is found in the texts of Dudley, 4th Lord North (1602–77). Like Patrick Cary's verses, some of Lord North's writings were printed after his death, but only after they had enjoyed several decades of literary life in script form. His verse and prose works, of which at least three compilation copies were made, were created over 1666 and 1667 by North's wife, Ann, with his knowledge and approval. North's twentieth-century editor, Dale Randall, dates one version, the Perkins manuscripts, as being made in the 1670s, just prior to the author's death in 1677; a shorter version had been sent to his son John early in 1667—on the volume's arrival, John wrote to thank his mother and to express the hope that his father would do likewise with his prose writings.[22] The last dated poem in the Perkins manuscripts is 1663, the last prose piece 1666. As Randall notes, it is a substantial volume of work with 148 pages of writing (all on the rectos of the leaves); the other volume, which was sent to son John, is calculated by Randall to consist of 118 recto and verso leaves of text.

Like Herbert Aston's wife, Lady North was responsible for turning her husband's scattered literary productions into long compilation volumes. Her son Roger said of her, "She not only wrote over whatever her lord had for the entertainment of his solitude composed into books, but kept strict accounts of all the household affairs and dealings whatsoever" (quoted in Randall, 165). In the opening declaration, North thanks his wife and offers a context for the pieces that follow in the volume. "Since freely of your selfe you have taken a resolution, to coppy out these imperfect essays of myne in the way of poetry, and soe to give them a fayrer character, than otherwise they can deserve," North begins,

> it now becomes fitt that I should give you some accompt of theyr condition,
> least those few besydes your selfe (for they were never designed to bee made

publike) whoe shall come to have a view of them should to the reading bring
an expectation too much to theyr disadvantage. . . . The truth is that a rap-
sody, or masse of things, soe different in nature, and composed at tymes of
lyfe, and coniunctures soe abhorrent one from the other, can very hardly ap-
peare good, and the rather because theyre Author, as hee was noe wayes by nature designed to Appollo his lawrell, soe hee never affected the honor to at-
tayne it; and where there is noe ambition, there can hardly arise perfection.
(128)

In describing his literary career, North notes that some of the early poems
really should not survive to see the light of day without correction by some
"lesse partiall penn then myne, if not to bee quite obliterated." Other more
serious poems, written later in his life, were "born" upon some "sadd occasion, or else upon a burden of perplexed thoughts, the very being delivered
(a terme well known to you Ladyes) could not but bring with it, much ease
and satisfaction to mee the Parent." Still other poems, "light and slight
enough for recreation," explore imaginary "obiects of Love," while some of
them are "not without a reall obiect, nor were it iniurious to any, if you
should assume it to your selfe, to bee the person intended."

In describing the collection of his lifelong works, North continues the
metaphor of childbirth by extending the application to the subsequent construction of volumes by his wife.

> But for the collection it selfe, such as it is, you may take it to you as your own,
> if you please, and peradventure with lesse censure (at least from some) then
> hath fallen upon those Ladyes, whoe out of an abundant affection, have called
> home theyre husbands spurious chyldren; for though this may bee taxed for
> levity in some parts, yett I hope, it will not bee found guilty of impurity,
> eyther in the conception, or exspression, and the chyld is as motherless, as Mi-
> nerva her selfe. You may safely there, do it the honor to own it, and not un-
> fittly as I thinke, for in a true sence all may been termed yours, that properly
> belongs to him, whoe is and delights to bee
>
> Entirely and constantly yours. (128–29)

The nature of the compilation—placing his work in a fairer "character," the
nurturing of his "spurious" poetic offspring in the production of a "domestic" volume—is wittily enriched by the metaphor. There is no indication
that Lady North contributed her own poems to the collection or exercised
editorial prerogative in the ordering or altering of his verse.

Although North states that the poems were not "designed" to be made public, the three volumes became public objects. Randall speculates that one of the volumes, the Perkins manuscripts, served as the base text for the posthumous publication of North's essay *Light in the Way to Paradise* (1682), the verse sections of the volume being sealed closed by strips of paper and sealing wax and the prose sections being soiled and marked by black printer's ink (103–4). North's oldest son, Charles, to whom two of the volumes are addressed (the Rougham Hall and Perkins manuscripts), published some of his father's prose pieces (as North had done for his father); Charles' brother Roger recorded in a manuscript preface to his *Life* that their father wrote

> divers slight Essays, and some verses, wch he tituled Light in the way to Paradise. These 2 last, his eldest son caused to be published with his name to it, viz. Dudley the 2d (misprinted for the 2d Dudley) Lord North. These were at first designed to remain with his family in MSS, and not to be published, but there is no harm done.[23]

It is interesting to speculate, first, how he could know the intention of the author that the multiple manuscripts remain in the family, especially given the family history of posthumous publications, and, second, what "harm" he envisioned might arise from family literature being made public property.

These issues—of whether a text was "designed" to be "Publicke" and what "harm" could be anticipated by a script author appearing in print— are only a few of the challenges facing the literary historian attempting to understand literary culture in the later seventeenth century. When confronted by assertions such as North's concerning his lack of intention to make his text "publicke," we have traditionally felt that (1) such statements are classic examples of private or closet writing, "aristocratic," dilettante literature, insignificant in terms of literary history because the texts formed no school, or (2) by preserving his manuscripts and by permitting several compilations of them, North had already imagined a more general readership, even if it is not, as in Habermas's model of a public sphere, where access is guaranteed to all citizens.

If we accept the first interpretation, we must then dismiss the literary activities and contributions of most of the writers of the early and mid-seventeenth century. We would have to reconfigure our perceptions of canonical authors including Cowley, Waller, Suckling, and Lovelace, all of whom participated in this type of manuscript literary culture before printing their texts. We would likewise have to rethink where we place in our notion of authorship writers such as Anne Bradstreet and Katherine Philips, whose texts appeared without their authorization, or Thomas Traherne and Anne Killigrew, whose texts were published after their death.

Although the 1620s and 1630s may be described by several critics as the "golden age of MS verse compilation," the practice obviously by no means vanished in the 1650s and well up through the early 1700s, even for authors not engaged in exchanging satires and lampoons.[24] As Marotti observes, the Restoration significantly changed the sociopolitical context of manuscript transmission and compilation (69), and, indeed, parts of the Cary manuscript volume compiled in the 1650s with its anti-Cromwell satires might have had a more difficult time being printed at that time; however, if its author had sought a printer, we do find anti-Cromwell pieces making their way from manuscript volumes into print during that same period, so politics may not have been the only factor influencing the mode of transmission.[25] On the other hand, there are a host of practical advantages for the provincial writer of using script rather than print to circulate his or her writings, whether the topic was controversial or banal.

Obviously, this type of manuscript text, whether a volume of verse or a single poem, could be created by a single individual in his or her home. For an example of a single author's use of scribal literary practices, we find that in 1699 Marie Burghope, the vicar's daughter living in Ashridge, Buckinghamshire, sent to the Lady Mary Egerton a manuscript fair copy of "The Vision: Or A Poeticall View of the Ashridge in the County of Bucks., The Ancient Seat of the Right Honorable John Earl of Bridgewater. Together with the History & Characters of the most considerable Members of that Noble Family."[26] In her opening epistle to Lady Mary (in which she spiritedly defends women's need to be educated in the same fashion as men), she gives some information about her own practice of authorship. "I love to recreate my selfe at leasure Hours with [the Muses'] Company. Tis sure as lawfull & laudable as our ordinary Chatt, telling of news & Backbiteing . . . putting our Selves into a Posture of Talkeing Nonsence in the Mode & other the admir'd Qualifications of our Sex." Burghope describes the twenty-five-page-long country house poem as being the product of "my Spare Hours . . . [on] a noble subject, & deserv[ing] the most judicious Pen." The subject matter filled her mind with inspiring thoughts, announced the author: "While I wrote, I swam with the tide of Fancy and the Waters under me were Boyant, I felt an unusuall Power to carry on the Description and to bring it to that Perfection you see it now before you."

She concludes her dedication to Lady Mary by saying that she is sure Lady Mary will excuse and appreciate this excursion into authorship, which "I plead it has been always my darling Talent," because of Lady Mary's qualifications as a judicious reader, "knowing that you, as well as all other, much admire and delight in Poesie, (tho their Genius Inclines them not to make it their Business)." For Marie Burghope, living in her father's house in a provincial town, her "business" was poetry, although her mode of authorship does not correspond to our current assumptions about either women's literary lives or the supposedly natural dominance of new technology over the old "business" of literary production.

This attractive text remains in its original fair copy manuscript form, now in the Huntington Library. Its author never experienced—nor, it seems, desired to experiment with—the new technology of print and in no way designed her text as a *publi*cation, scribal or otherwise. Burghope's text was, however, written and reproduced to be read by a learned and critical audience outside her own family circle. The physical characteristics of the piece and also its contents are a manifestation not only of the existence of a provincial literary community that delighted in poetry but also of the way in which a woman's "leisure hours" could be devoted to composing verse and to a dedicated reading of it.

One obvious conclusion that can be drawn from even these limited examples of scribal authorship and the manuscript text in its social context is that our definitions of "public" and "private" sit awkwardly with the particulars of the readership of manuscript texts. We traditionally have used "public" in the sense of meaning "published" and "private" in the sense of "personal." Here, we have texts whose readership was controlled through physical access to them rather than censorship imposed from an external agency and which was limited by the author's design, no matter (as we shall see in the discussion of literary piracy) how imperfect the control mechanisms actually were. On the other hand, they were not "private" in the sense that their readership was restricted only to God and the author, or even to the author's immediate family. What we tend to see is a "private" mode that, by its very nature, is permeated by "public" moments of readership, when the text is circulated and copied. The text, although not universally available to any purchasing reader, nevertheless engages in a "social" function.

An example of the intertwined nature of the private/public/social spheres can be seen in a manuscript volume compiled by Elizabeth Brackley and Jane Cavendish, the daughters of William Cavendish, the duke of Newcastle, by his first wife.[27] I have previously used that text to interrogate the then popular critical terms to describe women's writings as *closet texts,* which were viewed as "entirely private forms of writing not destined for publication and dealing with what limited experience might come within the circumference of a lady's life."[28] What the contents of this so-called closet manuscript volume demonstrated, however, was that the text was clearly a "social" one: a collaborative production, designed to please a reasonably extensive audience. Instead of being a defiant or subversive act, these pieces serve as a formal effort to confirm threatened social values and relationships.

By collapsing "public" into "publication," we seriously misconstrue the literary practices of such women and overlook the importance of the social function of literature for women as well as men writing in the so-called Cavalier tradition. In Earl Miner's analysis of male verse written in the Civil War years, in particular the poetry of friendship, poetry "sustains and continues the little society of the good few, and it demonstrates as well powers of mind and feeling"; this is also the model of social verse found in this "closet" volume.[29] Although Miner does not in his discussion consider either the practice of circulating verse in manuscript or the participation of women other than as subjects of such verse, his analysis of the choice of subject and genre underlines the central importance of being an author and of being a "good" reader during the mid-seventeenth century. This type of social function goes far beyond what Love calls "bonding" through the formation of a literary clique through exclusion (*Scribal Publication,* 180) and looks instead at the extent to which intellectual and literary life, as well as politics, was created, invigorated, and sustained through the writing and reading of script texts.

Kathryn R. King has more recently used this concept of the "social text" to analyze Jane Barker's *Poetical Recreations* (1688) and to reconstruct the young woman's circle of readers.[30] King finds that "far from being alienated, eccentric, tormented, or—in another version of the romantic narrative—a lonely voice from the periphery, Barker was engaged in literary exchange with a number of fellow poets, including at least three Cambridge students and (probably) a London bookseller" before the poems were published without her consent in 1687 (563). King concludes that for Barker, a "youngish unmarried woman," writing poetry and exchanging it "was a social as well as an intellectual act, an opportunity to exercise the mind, talents, and personality in acts of textual sociability" (563). The cases of Burghope, Cavendish, Brackley, and Barker, from quite different social backgrounds and under quite different circumstances of composition, show a similar pattern: the manuscript text operates as a medium of social exchange, often between the sexes, neither private nor public in the conventional sense of the terms, and a site at which women could and did comment on public issues concerning social and political matters.

It is important to note here (in contrast to Love's suggestion) that manuscript culture was not the province of women, in opposition to print culture as being the domain of men. In the examples of the university student John Chatwin and the almost monk Patrick Cary, and from Lord North to Mr. Hooper of Devon, it becomes clear that this type of authorship was equally attractive to both sexes and to a range of social classes. The dynamic network of writer and reader that in my view characterizes manuscript literary culture and social authorship is created by the process of being an author rather than by the production of a single text, in Eisenstein's terms, one capable of being fixed, attributed, and catalogued. Likewise, a reader in a manuscript culture, with a fluid text constantly subject to change, is responsible for participating in literary production as well as consumption; it is interesting to note here, too, how often the role of the reader of manuscript text becomes conflated with the roles of editing, correcting, or copying the text and extending its circulation of readers.

This is a type of authorship quite far removed from the characterization of it given by Kernan as aristocratic and authoritarian. Indeed, script authorship permitted a middle-class woman living in a small village, such as Marie Burghope, to have a cultivated audience, allowed Jane Barker to have literary connections with Cambridge and London, and created a means through which the teenage student John Chatwin was in literary exchange with the older, established author Nathaniel Wanley. One reason we associate manuscript author practices with "aristocrats" is because there was, pragmatically, a higher chance of these texts surviving for several generations and thus of being recovered. Manuscript texts have a much better chance of being preserved and passed down if their authors had established family homes or residences.[31]

Scottish memoirist Sir John Clerk, in preparing his manuscript, recognized this significance of the family library as the appropriate repository of scribal texts. On the cover of the manuscript volume chronicling his life from 1676 to 1755 he placed the blunt admonition, "I absolutely prohibit and discharge any of my Posterity from lending [these memoirs] or dispersing them abroad. They are to remain in the House of Pennicuik"—a condition for reading them he felt so strongly about that he also placed it on the title page of the manuscript volume.[32] This does not mean that only those with family libraries and family seats practiced manuscript authorship, but the examples of Burghope and Clerk do suggest that one must look in different places, and in different ways, to recover manuscript activities among middle- and lower-middle-class writers.

For example, posthumous editions can also reveal the prior existence of the material's manuscript circulation. The Quaker Mary Mollineux circulated her verses in manuscript for several years before her death.[33] She wrote poetry that dealt with a mixture of religious topics and contemporary poetic themes; several poems recall Katherine Philips' characteristic handling of the bonds of human friendship and the pain of parting. Mollineux also explores the notion of the retreat from a hostile, unjust society into the company of believers:

> Ah, let thy tender Care preserve and keep
> Us, with an Eye that is not part to sleep,
> But always guard thy little Heritage,
> From all their Adversaries, in this Age.
> ("The Retreat, a Meditation," 46)

Mary Mollineux met her husband, Henry Mollineux, when they were both imprisoned at Lancaster Castle; the volume opens with the testimony of the events of her life and sufferings as a Quaker by her cousin Frances Owen and her friend Tryall Ryder, which places her use of the Neoplatonic themes seen in Philips in a different social context.

In the prefatory materials of the posthumous edition, we get a glimpse of the nature of her practice of authorship. In Ryder's account, Mollineux is clearly a conscious, practicing author, but one not interested in taking advantage of the new print technology, even though the Quaker women as a

group were prolific publishers.[34] Ryder, whose acquaintance with Mollineux preceded her marriage in 1685, recalls:

> Several Years ago, when she was a single Woman, upon the Perusal of some
> Copies of her Verses, which she gave me, I felt such Unity of Spirit with them,
> that I said, I thought they might be of Service, if made Publick in Print;
> but she was not then free, that her Name should be exposed; she not seek-
> ing Praise amongst Men, but to communicate the exercise of peculiar Gifts
> amongst her near Friends and Acquaintance. (sig. A7v)

Ryder's use of the phrase "near Friends and Acquaintance" to encompass
Mollineux's readership is interesting, drawing attention to the way in which
one's "acquaintance," although distinct from those related by blood or marriage and from "near Friends," nevertheless is not considered "public." In
Mollineux's particular situation, she would have had perhaps even a better
access to having her works printed than Marie Burghope, given the activity
of the Quaker printers and also the large number of women involved in
Quaker printing. However, like Burghope, Mollineux chose a form of authorship and audience in which she controlled the production and circulation of the text and, like the earlier example of the aristocratic Cavendish
sisters, used her writings to cohere social bonds among like-minded readers.

In conclusion, these examples suggest several adjustments we must make
in our understanding of literary culture at large in the latter part of the seventeenth century. First, we must reconsider our assumptions about who
participated in manuscript writing and reading: manuscript circulation was
not confined to "aristocrats" and courtiers, although obviously practiced by
them, and it was not identified as being primarily female activity, either,
even at the end of the seventeenth century after the increased availability of
cheap print and publishers. As we have seen in the examples of the Aston,
Cary, and North families, male authors participated with enthusiasm in the
creation of social texts for their circles of family and friends. Nor, indeed,
was manuscript literary circulation restricted to poetry or short pieces. In
this essay, we saw the posthumous publication of Dudley North's essays by
his son, and in the following essay, we will find similar patterns of authorship in the example of Ralph Thoresby, for whom, for most of his life, manuscript transmission was the preferred mode of transmittal for a variety of
scientific, antiquarian, and political treatises.

One of the problems with our existing literary histories is that our current modes of analyzing authorship do not deal with this type of author who had no desire to publish or to "go public," except to form theories to explain the motivation behind what *we* see as authorial self-destruction. In our existing formulas for talking about the author, such an individual who wrote but did not intend to publish must have either been prevented from considering publishing by various social powers (whether national politics or domestic), as in J. W. Sanders' thesis concerning male Tudor courtier poets, or was so unskilled that no printer could be found to meet the author's unfulfilled need.

Even more telling, despite the excellent studies of the practice in the earlier seventeenth century and the recognition of the continued existence of the practice in the latter part of it, we still evaluate whole generations of early modern authors on the basis of their publication records. Students are introduced to the early seventeenth century with a description of literary activity and authorship that is clearly based on print as the marker of evaluation. One standard textbook depicts the literary climate for seventeenth-century women as bleak: "not even fine ladies were always sure of their spelling and punctuation," and except for letters and diaries, women writers' "contributions to belles-lettres were not many."[35] Here, examples such as Margaret Cavendish, who because of her "great wealth and social privilege" was "less inhibited from writing and publishing," are immediately contrasted by "Lady Mary Wroth, [who,] after one rash act of publication, was silenced for the rest of her life." The final observation before a student finally encounters the poems is that "though women struggled (and with only partial success) to find voices of their own, the age to come would speak more assuredly because of them" (1:1079).

In this 1993 example of literary history's treatment of gender and authorship, several important points should be noted. First, there is no indication in the account that fine gentlemen also had problems with spelling and punctuation according to modern standards because there was no standardized scheme of either spelling or punctuation. There is no indication that men who were contemporaries of the women cited also did not publish all of their texts. Finally, having a "voice" is equated with being in print, with the obvious implication that "work" is equated with print texts and anything else, manuscript copy in particular, is only "silence." The sole criterion of the success of these generations of women writers is the amount they *published,* with no mention of the amount they actually *wrote.* Intentionally or not, we thus train our students to classify literary activity with print as the superior mode and to employ false gender dichotomies when interpreting early modern texts.

As suggested by the examples of the Aston, Cary, and North families, along with the studies of individuals such as Mollineux and Burghope, manuscript authorship was still a flourishing feature of literary life in the later seventeenth century well into the early eighteenth. In these examples, we can find suggestions for further investigation; although the odds of a manuscript text's or volume's survival increased if it became part of a significant family's library, prefaces and printer's notes found in posthumous editions also indicate texts with more humble social origins. Suffice it to say, at this preliminary stage of the process of description, that literary life in late-seventeenth-century Britain included for both readers and writers the presence of scribal copies in competition with printed texts, texts their authors had no desire to have printed and for which we as critics have yet to create an accurate vocabulary, much less a complete description. What the literary history of the so-called Restoration and early Augustan periods still needs is an investigation of the ways in which earlier modes of literary transmission still shaped authors' practices and readers' perceptions and a more flexible definition of the nature of "public," "private," and "social" modes of authorship.

TWO

Literary Pirates and
Reluctant Authors

Some Peculiar Institutions
of Authorship

The best we can say for our selves is, that if we have injured you it is meerly in your own defense, preventing the present attempts of others, who to their theft would (by their false copies of these Poems) have added violence, and some way have wounded your reputation.   "To the Writer," RICHARD MARRIOTT and HENRY HERRINGMAN, printers of *Poems, Elegies,* to its author, Henry King

I feare the displeasure of no person in the publishing of these Poems but the Author's, without whose knowledge, and contrary to her expectation, I have presumed to bring to publick view what she resolved should never in such as manner see the Sun.   JOHN WOODBRIDGE on the publication of Anne Bradstreet's *The Tenth Muse* (1650)

One of the most peculiar aspects of authorship in this period of transition from manuscript culture to print must be the seeming danger of having one's works appear in print without one's knowledge, consent, or oversight. As academic authors, we labor to persuade journals and presses at least to consider the possibility of printing our works; the irony of writers in the 1650s through the early eighteenth century having to worry about presses being so eager for their texts that they would be willing, in effect, to steal them strikes one as an almost desirable aspect of the supposedly antiquated world of the manuscript author and his or her social text.

However, what do we know about the details of how manuscript texts were transformed without their authors' knowledge, participation, or consent into print ones? Current discussions about authorship in the late seventeenth and early eighteenth centuries engrossed in analyzing the presence or absence of the author function give little consideration to the practical difficulties of becoming a print author, even when that individual deliberately chooses that technology. We also lack concrete, specific accounts of material reading practices that did not involve print texts and a corresponding concept of audience for social rather than commercial texts. For example, as we have already observed, even the critical vocabulary used to discuss those aspects of manuscript culture that overlap (or in this instance, collide) with print practices reflects the bias towards print as the superior technology. The whole notion of "piracy," its source and the implications of the selection of such a term, is worth considering, as it may affect our perceptions of early modern authors and readers.

In addition to evaluating the nature of the critical discussion of such authors and the terminology we use to describe and analyze such acts of piracy, we need to reconsider the reactions and responses of the authors whose texts were published without their permission. Their complaints, whether disingenuous or sincere, are illuminating and reveal still further insight into the nature of manuscript authorship in contrast to print. Fortunately, a range of examples of authorial outrage exists for comparison from the period leading up to the development of copyright law and even well into the 1720s, as we shall see in the following essay's examination of Alexander Pope's relationships with both the print and manuscript culture of the early eighteenth century.

There are several aspects to this phenomenon of "forced" publication I wish to consider in terms of their effects on our perception of the literary culture of the period. Let us begin with the very terminology we have invented to describe the supposed activity: the *pirated* text, stolen from the author and printed without the author's knowledge or consent, and its twin phenomenon, the practice called *surreptitious publication,* in which the author lies about his or her desire to be in print. Both descriptive terms reinforce the perception that the world of the early modern writer and reader was a print one and that the principal motivation behind being an author was publication, even if unacknowledged. The very choice of language, too, reinforces an unstated narrative about the lives of early modern authors, that they were simply shy—or incompetent—sitting at home, waiting for the literary "pirate" to come and capture their texts and liberate them from their isolated towers into the romance of publication.

If we accept the fiction implicit in the term *piracy*, then how did such literary theft actually take place? Could one buy "hot" poetry at a dubious shop? Was there a special class of burglar devoted to lifting verse? Delightfully, there are some anecdotes that do support this scenario. Francis Quarles' widow, Ursula, revealed a rather shocking tale in her preface to an edition of *Judgement and Mercie for Afflicted Souls* (1646), informing her "Courteous Reader" that during her husband's last sickness

> this small Essay (the Epitome of his ejaculatory soul) was then taken from him by a slie hand, and presently printed without his knowledge; so that, as in like cases it always happens, it came forth much unsuitable to the Authour's mind, both in the form and the matter of it.[1]

In order to counter this theft by a "slie hand," she declares, "Though I cannot restore to him his lost treasure to itself again, [I am] putting it out so as that it now answers his own directions, and reforms many mistakes of the former Plagiary" (preface). It is significant that in Ursula Quarles' understanding of the practice of authorship the shift to print technology resulted in a less perfect "representation" of the author than that in the script, "both in the form and the matter." Equally interesting to note in this example, too, is that the subsequent preparation of an "authorized" text—literally a text prepared by the author for print—is thus the result of a desire to kill or nullify the pirated edition. It is not the author's desire to bring to life a script text or to bring acclaim to his or her life as an author, or to find an audience.

An equally brazen theft of manuscripts apparently befell Henry King, whose *Poems, Elegies* appeared in 1657 and which features a letter not from the author to the reader but from the printers to the author. They realize that King "will look on this publication with Anger which others must welcome into the world with Joy."[2] They then explain at groveling length, "The best we can say for our selves is, that if we have injured you it is meerly in your own defense, preventing the present attempts of others, who to their theft would (by their false copies of these Poems) have added violence, and some way have wounded your reputation" ("To the Writer"). The printers, Richard Marriott and Henry Herringman, optimistically conclude, "In hope of your pardon we remain, Your most devoted servants."

Again, one is struck by the connection between print and bad copies, between print and the distortion or deformation of the literary, social author.[3]

Such apologies and explanations from Marriott and Herringman appear in other volumes, too. In 1663, the same team announced in their edition of Abraham Cowley's verses: "Most of these Verses, which the Author had no intent to publish, having been lately printed at Dublin without his consent or knowledge, and with many, and some gross mistakes in the Impression, He hath thought fit for his Justification in some part to allow me to reprint them here."[4] Marriott and Herringman reveal the negative aspects of print technology—imperfect, incorrect copy that does not involve the author—and simultaneously place it as the only remedy to the print-created problem. Ironically, the author's involvement in yet another print production is the only way in which corrupt texts can be rescued from the literary pirates.

An interesting case for thinking about authorship and publication in the 1650s that involves issues not only of gender but also of geographic location is found in the publication history of Anne Bradstreet's poetry and prose. Bradstreet (1612–72), who had immigrated with her family to America in 1630, grew up in a family for whom literary activities were a part of their social and family fabric in ways not dissimilar to those of the North family. Her father, Thomas Dudley, steward to the earl of Lincoln at one time, was known to his contemporaries as a competent poet: Cotton Mather's biography of him notes that "he had an excellent pen, as was accounted by all; nor was he a mean poet; mention is made by some of his relations of a paper of verses, describing the state of Europe in his time, which . . . passed the royal test in King James's time."[5] According to contemporary accounts, Dudley even had "a bit of valedictory doggerel said to have been found in his pocket after his death" (White, 179). In her own poetry, Bradstreet makes references to her father's verses, especially in one of her earliest signed and dated poems, "To Her Most Honoured Father Thomas Dudley Esq these humbly presented," in which she hopes that her poetic exploration of the "four parts of the world" will harmonize with his.

After the Dudley and the Bradstreet families' move to America, it is clear that Anne pursued her poetic interests throughout her adult life, writing poems to relatives on particular occasions such as the birth of children, the departure of a beloved spouse, and the death of friends and family. She was also working on an epic account of the history of the monarchies of the world before the coming of Christ, based apparently on Raleigh's *History of the World,* which, according to White, involved a ten-year span of labor (229). The first of her surviving datable compositions appears to be "Upon a Fit of Sickness, Anno. 1632," and her last, "As weary pilgrim, now at rest," was created in 1669.[6] During this thirty-year span, in addition to writing prose meditations for her children, which were not published until the nineteenth century, she was apparently also reading her poetry to family and friends; we know, for example, that her sister Mercy, her brother-in-law Benjamin Woodbridge, and her son Samuel were poets,[7] a social group that Rosenmeier characterizes as "not simply family and close friends—indispensable to life in a small community; they were also a significant audience for poetry. They composed an important part of the intellectual group that nurtured Bradstreet's talents" (131).

It is clear from such biographical evidence that Bradstreet, like the members of the North and Aston families, actively participated in literary culture while far away from the center of literary production in London, with her poems read in manuscript and circulated in multiple copies. How they came to be printed, apparently without Bradstreet's knowledge, and her response to the printed text entitled *The Tenth Muse* are both interesting in this context.

Her response was correctly predicted by the author of the epistle to the reader, who is generally agreed to be her brother-in-law John Woodbridge, who had traveled back to London in 1649. Woodbridge's initial concern is to affirm to the reader that "it is the Work of a Woman, honoured, and esteemed where she lives, for her gracious demeanor, her eminent parts, her pious conversation, her courteous disposition, her exact diligence in her place, and discreet managing of her family occasions" and that, furthermore, "these Poems are the fruit but of some few hours, curtailed from her sleep, and other refreshments" (quoted in White, 255). The author, who had her verses printed "without [her] knowledge, and contrary to her expectation," never intended that they be read "in such a manner"; Woodbridge explains, however, "I found that divers had gotten some scattered papers, affected them well, were likely to have sent forth broken peices to the Author's prejudice, which I thought to prevent, as well as to pleasure those that earnestly desire the view of the whole." In White's opinion, Woodbridge "acted as a member of a sort of family conspiracy, in which Thomas Dudley and Simon Bradstreet supported [Woodbridge] in taking, without her knowledge, a step of great significance to the life of their close relative" (256).

Again, it is worth noting the contemporary insistence that the only reason the poems were printed was to protect the author from *other* imminent print texts, based on corrupt script copies. Obviously, Bradstreet's verses were read, circulated, and copied in manuscript over several decades—the 1650 volume includes poems dated as early as 1638 ("An Elegy upon Sir Philip Sidney") and 1642–43 ("A Dialogue between Old England and New"), up to "David's Lamentation for Saul and Jonathan" generally dated as 1649. Given the numerous commendatory verses that preface the printed volume, it is also clear that when Woodbridge and his family transported her texts with them to England the texts were circulated in script among Woodbridge's Oxford acquaintances.

Critics differ in their views about whether Bradstreet had envisioned a print audience for her manuscript texts. White declares that "if Anne Bradstreet had been in a position to supervise their publication she would undoubtedly have arranged them differently" (253). This agrees with the position taken by Rosenmeier, who adds, "There can be little doubt that she lost control of her drafts at that point and that changes were made that she did not know about until some years later when she saw the book in finished form" (131). In contrast, however, Amore points to "Prologue to the Tenth Muse" as "not the words of a humble, defenseless woman as some critics suggest. The entire prologue is meant to serve as introduction to a book of verses; it is an appeal, both clear and traditional by the author for a proper audience for her poetry" (xxv–xxvi).

In the poem "To my deare Sister, the Author of these Poems," Woodbridge admits "'Tis true, it doth not now so neatly stand, / As if 'twere pollisht with your owne sweet hand; / 'Tis not so richly deckt, so trimly tir'd / Yet it is such as justly is admir'd." Bradstreet recorded her own response to the printing of her poems in a piece included in the posthumous edition *Several Poems* (1678), "The Author to her Book," which also focuses on the unpolished, unprepared appearance of the poems in print in *The Tenth Muse* in contrast to their original script presentation.

> Thou ill-form'd offspring of my feeble brain,
> Who after birth did'st by my side remain,
> Till snatcht from thence by friends, less wise then true,
> Who thee abroad, expos'd to publick view,

Made thee in raggs, halting to th'press to trudg,
Where errors were not lessened (all may judg)
At thy return my blushing was not small,
My rambling brat (in print) should mother call.

(White, 267)

Bradstreet continues this poem describing her attempts to "Thy blemishes amend, if so I could," concluding, "'mongst Vulgars mayst thou roam / In Critick hands, beware thou dost not come." Based on such comments, critics have universally accepted that Bradstreet reworked *The Tenth Muse* with an eye to another edition in order to correct the mistakes of the "unauthorized" text. White thus envisions Bradstreet spending the next twenty-two years leading up to her death devoted to completing her long epic history and to "carefully revising her printed text in anticipation of another edition" (236).

The editor of the 1678 posthumous edition is generally believed to have been the future president of Harvard College, John Rogers. Rogers had married Bradstreet's niece Elizabeth and appears to have read Bradstreet's works in script as well as print, returning complimentary verses to her before her death.[8] Ironically, the posthumous edition, printed in Boston, perpetuates the masculine "piracy" of Bradstreet's texts, since it includes not only revised versions of poems in *The Tenth Muse* but also more materials found in her papers at her death, "which she never meant should come to publick view, amongst which, these following (at the desire of some friends that knew her well) are here inserted" (quoted in White, 361). Thus, whatever her intentions, Bradstreet herself never prepared a volume completely for print but instead appears to have spent much of her later poetic endeavors correcting the mistakes of her printed poems by creating other manuscript texts; there is no evidence of Bradstreet or her family negotiating with a printer or bookseller before her death for printing a corrected version. As we have seen in the previous examples, it appears that, until her death, print for Bradstreet was associated with corruption of the text and with a misrepresentation of the author.

This same fear of corrupt texts through unauthorized printing lies at the heart of the musician Henry Lawes' representation of his motive to seek publication himself. In his address to all "Understanders or Lovers of

MUSICK," Lawes brushes through the typical author's gestures of modesty ("It is easy to say I have been much importun'd by Persons of Quality, to Publish my Compositions . . . nor was I drawn to it by any little thoughts of private Gain") to launch an attack on publisher John Playford's 1652 volume containing Lawes' songs.[9] Lawes alleges in his opening that Playford had "lately made bold to print, in one Book above twenty of my Songs, whereof I had no knowledge till [Playford's] Book was in the Presse"; Lawes continued, "It seems he found those so acceptable that he is ready for more." Therefore, Lawes observes, "[The] Question is not, whether or not my Compositions shall be Publick, but whether they shall come forth from me, or from some other hand; and which of the two is likeliest to afford the true correct Copies, I leave others to judge." In addition to having the irritation of finding his own works incorrectly presented, Lawes declares, "I have often found many of mine that have walkt abroad in other men's names: how they came to lose their Relations and be Anabaptiz'd, I think not worth examining" (Evans, 199). Lawes had previously published a text—*Choice Psalmes* appeared in 1648 with supposedly the last portrait of Charles I on the title page—but that text was printed as a memorial to his recently deceased brother, William, "unfortunately lost in the unnaturall Warres," to ensure that "his greater Compositions, (too voluminous for the Presse) which I the rather now mention, lest being, as they are, disperst into private hands, they may chance be hereafter lost" (Evans, 178). In his preface to *Ayres and Dialogues,* Lawes is at pains to declare, "As for those Copies of Verse in this Book, I have rendered their Names who made them, from whose hands I received them" (Evans, 200).

Perhaps the most famous literary piracy in the Restoration period is that of a friend of Lawes', who, like King and Cowley, found herself confronting a pirated edition. The unauthorized edition of Katherine Philips' verse in 1664 is worth examining in light of how that particular event demonstrates the transition from manuscript to print text and how such an authorial event has been handled by subsequent generations of scholars. As I have discussed in an earlier study, many critics have treated Katherine Philips' pirated poetry as a classic study of the woman wronged, whereas I and other critics such as Elizabeth Hageman tend to see it as an author at odds with changing literary culture and technology.[10] Philips, who had had public performances of her dramatic translations and who contributed commendatory verse to Lawes' second printed volume, wrote quite angrily about the unauthorized volume of her poetry:

> 'Tis impossible for Malice it self to have printed those Rhymes, which you tell me are got abroad so impudently, with so much Wrong and Abuse to them, as the very Publication of them at all, tho' never so correct, had been to me, who never writ a line in my Life with the Intention to have it printed.[11]

This sounds quite similar to protestations we have seen made, by authors male and female who were active participants in a manuscript culture and thus did not apparently see a need to seek an unknown commercial audience for their texts.

As Hageman notes, Philips also specifically complained that the poems were "abominably printed" and that the volume included poems that were not hers (55). Hageman points out Philips' early comments regretting that she had permitted the printing of *Pompey* by John Crook, the king's printer in Dublin: "It was purely in my own Defence that I did; for had I not furnish'd a true Copy, it had been printed from one that was very false and imperfect" (47). This sounds remarkably like the justification Marriott and Herringman offered Henry King, which Herringman likewise offered to excuse his 1663 edition of Philips' friend Abraham Cowley's verses; it also sounds much like John Woodbridge's explanation for printing Anne Bradstreet's manuscripts.

Unlike her previous associations with print—her translation of Corneille's *Pompey,* which had been printed in 1663 by John Crook, her contributions to Lawes' printed volume, and her contribution to *Poems, by Several Persons* (1663) (which Hageman interestingly describes as "structured according to the same interactive principles that inform many manuscript miscellanies of the period. . . . The book images a coterie conversation among those five poets, several of whose poems complement one another" [48])—the printing of her collected verses in a single-author volume seemed to Philips inappropriate, both for the printed page and for commercial readership.

In her letters, it becomes clearer why, although her dramatic translations and her songs are fit for print, her collected verse is not. Booksellers wanted her verse for different reasons than did the original circle of readers for whom she wrote, those readers whose "Commands" inspired her to write.

As Elizabeth Hageman and Andrea Sununu observed, Katherine Philips was a "social" poet in the most traditional seventeenth-century manner: "her contemporary reputation owed much to manuscript circulation. Katherine Philips was a manuscript poet, a poet who circulated her verse in hand-written copies, who knew it would be rewritten and revised as it was recopied by others, who herself revised what she had earlier written."[12] The booksellers, however, did not rewrite and circulate her poems in the same manner or for the same purposes as did her manuscript readers: as in the case of Quarles and King, the printers produced flawed texts, unchecked by the author, in order "to entertain the Rabble," Philips' rather ruthless characterization of people who bought verse in print rather than participating directly in creating a literary culture (*Letters,* 230). Her songs, on the other hand, involved a close friendship with Lawes and his collaboration in the creation of the musical setting for them; the publication of the translation was a record of a social event, a public performance on stage in Dublin.

For Katherine Philips, print was thus not always a better technology for presenting her poetic works. Poetry in print produced only "indiscriminate" texts for indiscriminate readers, readers incapable of participating in the social literary world of Philips that Hageman and Sununu described. At her death, she, too, was preparing an authorized edition to negate the unauthorized, and it is illuminating to note not only the similarities of the events of the pirating of her texts and Lawes' compositions but also their nearly identical responses.

Jane Barker made a similar complaint that Benjamin Crayle had published some fifty of her poems in *Poetical Recreations* without her consent in 1688.[13] The full title of the printed volume makes interesting reading itself from the point of view of those interested in who printed what: *Poetical Recreations: Consisting of Original Poems, Songs, Odes, &c. With Several New Translations. In Two Parts. Part I. Occasionally Written by Mrs Jane Barker. Part II. By several Gentlemen of the Universities, and Others.* Based on Barker's response in an unpublished poem to her Cambridge friends on the appearance of the volume, King notes that "it is hard to know how to take Barker's claim that the *Poetical Recreations* verses were printed 'without her consent.' . . . [But] there is little reason to imagine her distressed by their publication" (King, "Jane Barker," 557). King notes that Barker's claim may be simply disingenuous, but even if sincere, it is open to numerous interpretations:

It could mean any of a number of things: that Barker knew of the venture and strenuously opposed it; knew and acquiesced with sadness; knew and concealed her boundless delight; did not know but was not greatly displeased in the event—the possibilities go on. (559)

King deduces that Barker's Cambridge male correspondents supplied the bookseller with copies of Barker's poems in addition to their own; it is interesting to note, too, that part 2 includes twelve poems by the publisher, Benjamin Crayle, in which he professes an acquaintance with Barker (who is addressed as "Galaecia" and "Cosmelia"). King notes that the "bookseller and poet were engaged in literary play of some kind" before the appearance of the volume, which suggests another source of manuscripts for the printed edition.[14] It is perhaps significant as well that, unlike the other examples of pirated authors, Barker makes no complaint at all about the quality of the texts and the correctness of them, which suggests perhaps that Barker had more confidence in the bookseller, in effect a literary colleague.

Around 1701, while living in exile in St. Germain with James II's court, Barker compiled a manuscript collection of her verse that re-creates her earlier coterie verses. On the title page of this manuscript miscellany, she informs the reader in some detail about the contents: "Poems on Several Occasions in three parts: The first referring to the times. The second, are poems writ since the author was in France, or at least most of them. The third, are taken out of a miscellany heretofore printed, and writ by the same author." In a headnote on the title page of this manuscript volume, Barker states that the contents of the third section had been published without her consent and that she is giving the correct versions in the manuscript text.[15] Thus, twelve years after the printed appearance of her poems, they are "reissued" by the author in manuscript form. In contrast to the fate of her early London poems, it is interesting to note that in addition to this three-part compilation volume of her manuscript verses, Barker at this time also prepared a separate manuscript volume of verse for the exiled Prince of Wales in 1700 that was never printed; as her editor Carol Shiner Wilson notes, these poems composed while Barker was living in France were intended for private circulation among sympathetic associates, in part to reinforce shared commitments among loyal Jacobites (*Galesia Trilogy*, xlii). Barker did later publish her fiction, which has interpolated verse—*Love Intrigues* (1713), *A Patch-work Screen for the Ladies* (1723), and *The Lining of the Patch-work*

Screen (1726)—but she never again printed any of her verses separately from these narratives.

King raises the whole issue of the "sincerity" of Barker's claim that her verse was pirated. Perhaps one could say that anyone who entered into "literary play" with a known bookseller should not be surprised by suddenly appearing in print. Part of the irony of the Katherine Philips example, of course, is that the printer protested that he believed that he did indeed have Philips' permission to print. To add further to the irony, the bookseller in question was none other than Richard Marriott, who penned the unabashed confession of the theft of Henry King's manuscript.[16] John Grismond, whom Nathan Tinker has identified as the printer of the text, was imprisoned not long after the Katherine Philips incident for illegally printing law books (Tinker, "John Grismond," 32). However, in the case of Philips, as Elizabeth Hageman has written, the bookseller Richard Marriott published on 18 January 1664 an announcement in the *Intelligencer* (the same publication that had previously, on 14 January 1664, announced the forthcoming volume by the "incomparable Madam *Cathrine Philips*") that Marriott was withdrawing the volume from sale, "but assuring readers that it had been his understanding that Philips's poems had come to him with her own permission."[17]

Was it the case of the biter bit, the bookseller deceived? Certainly, there is anecdotal evidence from other booksellers suggesting that they, too, could be in the dark about the provenance of the manuscript texts they handled. One of the most complete examples is provided by John Dunton's attempt to extricate himself from a minor publishing scandal. "The World may, perhaps, expect I should here say something of *The Second Spira*," admits Dunton in the course of his account of his practice as a bookseller, and his case is illuminating not only for what it shows about Dunton's sense of what would sell but also for relationships between authors and booksellers.[18]

In 1693, Dunton had published *A Second Spira*, supposedly the deathbed conversations of an avowed atheist, made from the notes taken by the attending clergyman. In his autobiography, Dunton is at some pains to lay out how the manuscript came to him and how the authorship was validated.

This Narrative was put into my hands by Mr. Richard Sault, the Methodizer, Dec. 26, 1692. Mr. Sault assured me, "he received the Memoirs, out of which he had formed the copy, from a Divine of the Church of England." He also confirmed the truth of it by a Letter and a Preface from the same Gentleman. The Letter ran thus:—"Sir, I had yours with the Manuscript, and having compared it with the Memoirs I took, I think you have done me, and the case of that miserable Gentleman, a rigid justice." (1:154)

The evidence seemed to Dunton to be further solidified by the presence of a "Preface" also supplied by the unknown clergyman, which stated, "Having examined the Piece, now it is perfected, with the original Notes and Papers, which I drew myself, I find the substance and material part very faithfully done; and I dare affirm that there is nothing material left out, nor are there any interpolations which are not genuine." Dunton titled the text *The Second Spira* to capitalize on the popularity of the original deathbed memoir of Francis Spira, an Italian lawyer who converted to Protestantism but who "finally yielded to the threats of the Roman Catholic Church, made a recantation, and thereby incurred certain destruction," a moving tale that had gone through thirteen English editions by 1695 and is mentioned by Bunyan in *Grace Abounding* (Parks, 57–58). *The Second Spira* did quite well for Dunton, and only three months after its original appearance, he advertised the fifth edition, with thirty thousand copies sold in six weeks (Parks, 58). The problem was, as rival booksellers such as Nathaniel Crouch began to protest, it was not an authentic narrative. No Reverend Sanders ever was found or came forward to testify concerning the validity of either the memoirs or the supporting letters and preface.

Although he defended the authenticity of the text at the time, in his later years Dunton came to the conclusion that, indeed, there was no dying atheist in despair but instead that Richard Sault himself was the author. Dunton reveals that, "a little before he wrote the Narrative, [Sault] was under the severest terrors of his own conscience; his despair and melancholy made him look like some walking ghost" (1:155). Dunton rebukes himself for not guessing at the time that Sault was the true author. Sault, according to Dunton, apparently wandered about Dunton's house uttering "broken speeches," exclaiming periodically, "I am damned! I am damned!," which alarmed Dunton's wife. In Dunton's estimation, Sault was in the exact same condition as the supposed second Spira and thus the perfect candidate for authorship: "it is hard to conceive how any man could write such a dismal narrative that did not himself feel what he there relates" (1:155). Did Dunton know before printing the text who the author of the manuscript was? If the answer is yes, it is a tribute to the mount of effort Dunton was willing to put into constructing a screen for Sault; if the answer is no, then we have another example of the ways in which print technology, rather than manuscript practice, could manipulate the reader's perception of the author, this time by the author himself for the purposes of concealment.

How have subsequent generations of historians dealt with this peculiar phenomenon of authors being printed without any desire to be so and printers who had no idea whose work they were printing? The term *piracy* associated with literary texts is probably most familiar to us because of Cyril Judge's *Elizabethan Book-Pirates* (1934) and studies such as Pollard's on the transmission of Shakespeare's play texts. Judge explains the legal definition of literary piracy as "the stealing of an author's work by reprinting it in full or in substantial part without the authority of the copyright proprietor, and is in fact an infringement at wholesale or otherwise of the author's exclusive right."[19] As Judge himself points out in his study, since copyright as we define it and as it is applied in this passage was unknown during Elizabeth's reign, the term is highly anachronistic—nevertheless, he continues to employ it and titles his study as such.

More recent critics have compounded the confusion by applying the copyright term to manuscript texts. As is clear in its definition, piracy refers to "reprinting" texts, which obviously assumes that the original would already exist in a print form. There is no mention of scribal or manuscript copy. H. P. Bennett, in his excellent book on books and readers in the first half of the seventeenth century, uses *piracy* routinely to describe the publication of manuscript texts: in the chapter entitled "Piracy," for example, he focuses on cases in which printers in the 1630s were printing manuscripts not only without their authors' consents but also, in some cases, without knowing who the authors were (59–66). This use of the term *pirated* is continued in less formal discussions of individual authors: student readers of anthologies are introduced to Katherine Philips with the information that, although she never intended to publish, a "pirated edition of rough copies of her poems" was printed in 1664.[20] Thus, traditional literary histories of the later seventeenth century have continued and incorporated an earlier term dealing specifically with the reprinting of commercial texts and transferred it unrefined in their description of manuscript activities.

Legally, while the "slie hand" that took Quarles' manuscript without his consent committed theft, the hand that set the print did not, since there were no copyright laws to protect the financial interests of the author at that time. It was not a theft of money, of being defrauded of potential income, therefore, I believe, that so angered Quarles' widow or Katherine Philips—it was the denial of the opportunity for the author to be involved in the process of production, an aspect over which the manuscript author had complete and often personal control. Furthermore, it was a denial, indeed, even of the necessity for the author to participate in the production of the print text, completely dissolving the tie between the author and his or her work. The result was a text that was no longer created by the author but instead by the bookseller. It is not in any sense a collaborative effort between editor, typesetter, and author, as described by Jerome McGann as characteristic of later periods' literary cultures.[21] Instead, it borders on the creation of rival versions of a literary text, one by the author and one by the printer.

By using terms such as *piracy*, which is derived from print culture for a manuscript phenomenon, I believe we have inflated a narrative of literary life in which no script was safe from the rapacious desire of a printer or bookseller, that even against the writer's will commercial print culture *would* have his or her text and violate his or her modesty, so dominant was this new technology. A perusal of the lists of manuscript holdings in the major British university libraries and in the great house libraries in England, Scotland, Wales, and Ireland quickly reveals that for the manuscript texts pirated during the seventeenth and early eighteenth centuries, many more remained safely in script.[22] Such manuscript texts—both single items and compiled volumes—extend our awareness of how Mary Hobbs' observation about the significance of the manuscript text in writing the literary history of the first part of the seventeenth century is still applicable when generalizing about literary culture and habits of writing and reading in the latter part of the century and in the beginning of the eighteenth.

The whole phenomenon of *piracy*, as awkward and anachronistic as that term is, however, does invite us to rethink our notions of the relationship between the writer and reader, the writer and technology. Paradoxically, for the poet in particular to have his or her works printed seems to have been a matter of first creating through print a corrupt text and then rescuing it with a second "authorized" print version that attempts to replicate the original scribal text. As we shall see in the subsequent essays, even authors who were personally involved in the production of their works had to deal with the problems of printers' errors and publishers' or booksellers' deliberate changes to their texts. As we have seen in these examples of authors who completely lost (or in the case of Barker, perhaps surrendered) control over their previously social texts as they became commercial ones, what is most frequently lamented is the loss of quality of the texts and the distortion or misrepresentation of the literary, social author's work.

THREE

The Very Early Career
of Alexander Pope

Lord Bolingbroke is much the best writer of the age.—Nobody knows half the extent of his excellencies, but two or three of his most intimate friends.

ALEXANDER POPE, quoted in Joseph Spence's *Anecdotes, Observations and Characters of Books and Men*

My Essay on Criticism was written in 1709; and published in 1711; which is as little time as ever I let any thing of mine lay by me.

ALEXANDER POPE, in *Anecdotes*

For a final case study that exemplifies the continuation of a tradition of manuscript authorship practices simultaneously with the author's heavy involvement with the world of print, let us consider an unlikely writer: Alexander Pope. For literary historians, Pope has always been associated with the power of print, the author who took full advantage of the blossoming of the publishing trade to secure a living for himself as a poet free from the constraints of a dying system of patronage and who, furthermore, outwitted the booksellers. "Among poets, of course," wrote Harry Ransom in "The Rewards of Authorship in the Eighteenth Century," Alexander Pope became the "type of literary success."[1] Pope is depicted by his most recent biographer, Maynard Mack, as the consummate commercial author, a "shrewd judge of timing and public taste."[2] John Butt declared that Pope never doubted "he was a classic," who wished to ensure his literary fame through publication, showing his "concern for his text and his canon by publishing The Works of Mr. Alexander Pope in magnificent quarto and folio."[3] What has gotten lost in the centuries of celebrating Pope as a literary free agent are his ties to the older tradition of circulating fair copy manuscripts and, indeed, his continued participation of the culture of manuscript authorship.

One reason for this lack of interest in Pope as a participant in an older tradition of authorship is easy and obvious: his later career provides a plethora of fascinating materials for the investigation of print culture. Pope was deeply involved in fashioning the financial relations between authors and booksellers, the practice of public subscription, and the development of copyright. It is not surprising that the majority of studies involving Pope's literary career have thus focused on his participation in print culture; the biographical and bibliographical details of Pope's involvement with the commercial world of letters has produced excellent, detailed studies.[4] David Foxon exhaustively reconstructs Pope's relationships with printers, publishers, and booksellers; Pat Rogers uses him to frame his analysis of Grub Street and the world of hack writers.[5] The publishing history of his letters, in particular, and his battles with Edmund Curll have proven to be fertile ground for studies by James Winn and others not only into the nature of correspondence as a literary genre but also into the legal status of an author's text.[6] Likewise, the success of the subscription publication of the *Iliad* (1715–20) and the *Odyssey* (1725–26), as well as the relative failure of *The Works of Shakespeare* (1725), provides excellent material for Pat Rogers' study of the demographics of literary subscription lists.[7] In short, Pope's career after 1715 has provided such marvelous materials for the study of print culture that even George Sherburn's classic study, *The Early Career of Alexander Pope,* views the primary significance of his preprint literary life as being an apprenticeship to the world of commercial writing, through the making of useful friends for subsequent publishing ventures.[8]

So much emphasis has been placed on Pope's links to the world of booksellers and dunces on the one hand and his own commercial success with the new technology of print on the other that we tend to assume he viewed print publication with the same sense of its superiority to manuscript exchange as we do. There is, after all, his famous dismissal of Dorset and Rochester as "holiday-writers; as gentleman that diverted themselves now and then with poetry, rather than as poets," made even worse by Spence's gloss that the remark was "said kindly of them; rather to excuse their defects, than to lessen their characters."[9]

Such dismissals, even if meant kindly, have been taken by his later critics as expressing his complete, final view of the nature and practices of coterie or social authorship. As we have seen in the previous essay, a stated preference for manuscript over print technology is often derided by later generations of critics as an affectation or a nostalgic anachronism. In Pope's case, interestingly, such supposed nostalgia becomes compounded by charges of authorial hypocrisy or just plain lying—as Mack states in his foreword to Cowler's edition of the prose works, the text offers a "fascinating even if depressing study of the art of lying, another art of which Pope was unfortunately a master" (viii).

As Sherburn notes at the opening of his study, "few writers have suffered more from prejudiced views of their personalities than has Pope. . . . Few will deny that Pope's supposed personality daily prejudices readers against his work" (v). As Sherburn noted about earlier generations of literary commentary on his poems, critics interested in the history of authorship and the printing trade tend to discount as part of his untrustworthy persona Pope's own ambivalent comments about his publications. Mack derides as laughable Pope's "aristocratic attitude towards the writer's profession . . . that crops out so incongruously from time to time in his statements about his work—that he wrote only because it pleased him" (*Life*, 110). Such "snobbery," Mack admits, is a "clinging to an ideal of serene detachment cherished by almost everyone in this age," but nevertheless, Mack implies that Pope's tendency to devalue his publications is, like his example from Congreve, "a disagreeable form of cant," a feature of Pope's perceived manipulative character. As James Winn sees it, "Pope liked to maintain the posture of the gentleman author, writing for the sake of truth and his own aristocratic friends, and . . . needed to cling to this fiction both psychologically and practically."[10] Indeed, it is Pope's assertions that he was a gentleman writing for gentlemen, not a commercial hack, that are commonly used to provide part of the psychological explanation for the "engineering" of the surreptitious publication of his letters and his reputation for deviousness in dealing with the agents of print culture.[11]

Even though his critics uniformly agree with the position taken by Mack that the publication of the *Pastorals* in 1709 was the event that "launched Pope on his public career as a poet," I would urge a reconsideration of the phrase "public career," given that Pope had already established a readership and a reputation as a poet before ever being published. Throughout Pope's life, while he wrote his translations and prepared editions with money foremost in mind, there remained other aspects of his activities as a poet that were designed for a controlled social audience and remained within the realm of the pattern of scribal authorship and audience. Furthermore, Pope's treatment of his manuscripts—what has been described as his constant revision of them, along with the existence of multiple print versions of the same text—suggests more the literary culture of the social, manuscript author than that of the commercial one.

There are numerous aspects of Pope's literary life that have caused disjointures in the accounts of his commercial career and the subsequent turn to his character (or lack thereof) as an explanation for the seeming inconsistencies. Perhaps another explanation for some of Pope's apparently disingenuous literary practices may lie in understanding his very early literary career from 1700 to 1715. For example, in treating Pope's early manuscripts, Sherburn observes that "concerning many of his juvenilia Pope adopted the wise procedure of talking—and destroying," which is certainly true at one level, although it does not engage the issue of the curious careers of those other early manuscript texts, with their multiple versions and multiple manuscript venues, and what these pieces suggest about Pope's practices of authorship (83). Sherburn, for example, cites as juvenilia Pope's "Ode to Solitude," which Sherburn states was written when the poet was twelve—but he also notes that it was not completed in its final form until the poet was forty-two (83–84). As Howard Erskine-Hill has observed in his study of Pope's relationship with the Caryll family, the poems and manuscripts produced before the 1715 translation of the *Iliad* "may suggest the usefulness to students of Pope of a closer investigation of his friends and contemporaries, irrespective of whether or not they were artists in their own right."[12]

Attention is usually paid to Pope's associations with writers such as Gay and Swift, writers deeply involved in print texts and publishing; we are less familiar with Pope's involvement with poets and readers who remained in the world of manuscript transmission. That Pope read an enormous amount of other people's poetry has long been known, texts not only by the Scriblerians but by a wide range of minor writers as well. The hyperbolic siege of the desperate hack writers that opens the "Epistle to Dr. Arbuthnot" makes it clear that Pope, like famous writers in all times, was approached after he was an established print author by total strangers to read, comment on, and correct their texts with the express purpose of having them printed for profit. Numerous studies have been written discussing Pope's relationship with the hack authors populating Grub Street whom he used so mercilessly in *The Dunciad*.[13] But what of those writers who had no desire to have their texts published—what was Pope's relationship with them? To what extent was Pope reading poetry not in print but in manuscript, and to what extent was Pope's verse composed for and enjoyed by a closed readership before it was fashioned for a general commercial one? There is no certain answer, but there are numerous indications that while subsequent generations of literary historians have viewed Pope as the embodiment of the new style of the modern publishing author, his reading and writing practices, especially during the first decades of the eighteenth century, were still closely associated with the practices of manuscript authorship and social literature rather than commercial.

The notion that the publication of *The Pastorals* by Tonson was the entrance into literary life for Pope is firmly entrenched as part of our image of Pope as a man for whom poetry was a profitable profession rather than a diversion, as for the "holiday poets" of the Restoration court. Sherburn characterizes publication as a rite of passage: "such publication certainly constituted a dignified and assured entry to the world of letters" (85). William Wycherley might seem to be agreeing with Sherburn when he commented more robustly to the young Pope that he approved of Pope's making Tonson his "Muses' Introductor into the world, or Master of Ceremonies," who had been "so long Pimp, or Gentleman-Usher to the Muses."[14] One could also argue, however, that in these two statements there is a difference in attitude towards breaking into print between the twentieth century's celebration of it as a literary coming of age and Wycherley's representation of the publisher as a pimp or walker to the muses, providing a good experience for the loss of young Pope's literary virginity. Pope's response to Wycherley on this occasion also plays with this imagery: Pope writes concerning publication that

> those who have once made their court to those Mistresses without Portions, the Muses, are never like to set up for Fortunes. . . . Jacob [Tonson] creates Poets, as Kings sometimes do Knights, not for their honour, but for money. Certainly he ought to be esteem'd a worker of Miracles, who is grown rich by Poetry.
>
> > What authors lose, their Booksellers have won,
> > So Pimps grown rich, while Gallants are undone.[15]

As Winn points out, such imagery makes the poet a "soldier of fortune," whose "mistresses, the muses, not only lack dowries but turn out to be prostitutes in the employ of a pimp: worse yet, that pimp is the bookseller" ("On Pope," 95).

The audience for the pastorals before Tonson "pimped" them is interesting because of its number and influence on the manuscript texts. According to Pope, the piece was begun around 1704 and circulated widely before being seen by Tonson in 1706 and finally printed in 1709. Apart from his neighbor Sir William Trumball, who seems to have watched over its composition from the start, we can see how such networks form by looking at Pope's correspondence with another Restoration literary figure, William Walsh. Although the exact date of Pope's acquaintance with Walsh is open to debate, it is clear that Pope sent pieces to Walsh for comment and correction. In one letter, Walsh gracefully assures the young man that he will be "very glad of the continuance of a correspondence" and concludes in a teasing vein that he will take pleasure "not only to read over the Verses I have now of yours, but more that you have written since; for I make no doubt but any one who writes so well, must write more" (Pope, *Correspondence*, 1:18).

Foxon agrees with Sherburn that Pope met Walsh, Wycherley, and Congreve in London about the same time, while visiting Will's Coffee House, Dryden's former literary site, a place where, according to the *Tatler*, in 1709 one "used to see songs, epigrams, and satires in the hands of every man" one met.[16] As the letter above suggests, Pope had initiated a correspondence with the older poet for the purpose of having Walsh read and comment on his manuscripts. Walsh was certainly not the only established reader Pope engaged in his composition of *The Pastorals*: Pope himself inscribed on particular fair copy of *The Pastorals* that it was the one seen by Congreve, Walsh, Garth, Halifax, Wharton, Dorchester, Buckingham, Mainwaring, Granville, Southern, Sir Henry Sheers, and "others" (*Correspondence*, 1:17 n. 1). The pastorals, thus, had quite an impressive critical readership for several years before they became commercially available; Jacob Tonson's famous letter to Pope is dated April 1706, and in addition to suggesting that the young poet did not immediately take him up on the offer, it also establishes the reputation of the manuscript text as such.

> Sir,—I have lately seen a pastoral of yours in mr. Walshs & mr Congreve's hands, which is extreamly fine & is generally approv'd off by the best judges in

poetry. I Remember I have formerly see you at my shop & am sorry I did not Improve my Acquaintance with you. If you design your Poems for the Press no person shall be more Carefull in the printing of it, nor no one can give a greater Incouragement to it. (*Correspondence*, 1:17)

There is some evidence to support Tonson's claim that Pope's manuscripts were approved by the "best judges" and that his reputation predated his supposed "entrance" into literary life. In 1707, two years before any of Pope's verse had been printed, William Wycherley teases Pope that the younger man's reputation makes the other young wits leery of him: "all men own, who have either seen your writings, or heard your discourse—enough, to make others show their Judgment, in ceasing to write, or talk especially to you, or in your company" (*Correspondence*, 1:30).

This fair copy of *The Pastorals* that Pope circulated was not a working draft. Pope, of course, became famous for his practice of never ceasing to correct a line, a practice to which I return later. Butt notes that this particular manuscript, like several others of Pope's that have been preserved, is a fair copy in his hand that carefully sets punctuation and spacing, giving the appearance of a printed page (550). Indeed, the excellence of the calligraphy causes Harold Love to argue that it proves that Pope "taught himself his script by imitating typography" and therefore, presumably, is also an example of a text that "wanted to be" print (37 n. 5). This is probably the manuscript that one of the above-listed gentlemen showed to Jacob Tonson; there is no reason to assume that they hid it from other interested readers whose names are not recorded by Pope on the text.

The same type of patterns emerge when one looks at the publication history of Pope's early pieces such as "Windsor-Forest" and "The Temple of Fame." "Windsor-Forest" was composed around 1704, but did not appear in print as such until 1713, apparently at the insistence of one of its manuscript readers, Lord Lansdowne (Spence, *Anecdotes*, 131). As several critics have demonstrated, in 1712 Pope revised the piece to suit a celebration of the Peace of Utrecht. What happened to it in the intervening years, however? From the existence of at least one early fair copy, we know it was being read. Interestingly, Pope wrote to Caryll early in 1713, before the poem's appearance in print, that he was "at the same time both Glad and ashamed to find (when [they] were at Old Winsor) that [Caryll] had more lines than one of that poem by heart" (*Correspondence*, 1:173).

When one begins looking, it is easy to discover numerous other texts that enjoyed an independent literary life in manuscript for many years before being printed. After his quarrel with Addison in 1715/16, Pope responded by creating the portrait of Addison as Atticus, which circulated widely for approximately three years before Addison's death in 1719 (Sherburn, 147–48); Spence records Pope's explanation of the conflict between himself and Addison in a conversation held 1734–36 and that "Dr. Trapp, who was by at the time of this conversation, said he wondered how so many people came to imagine that Mr. Pope did not write this copy of verses till after Addison's death: since so many people, and he himself for one, had seen it in Addison's life time" (106). The verse portrait would eventually find its place in "The Epistle to Dr. Arbuthnot," published in 1735.

As seen in the examples of "Windsor-Forest" and "The Epistle to Dr. Arbuthnot" (which is more closely examined later), Pope's practice of composing occasional pieces—which are sometimes labeled as fragments—that he then expanded or combined at a later date further complicates arriving at a clear sense of the time lapse between composition and publication. If one performs the duncelike task of calculating the years between composition and publication of Pope's works, even using the last possible dates for composition suggested by Ault and leaving out twenty-seven pieces published posthumously, one finds that the average delay between composition and print during Pope's life was just over six years. When one looks specifically at his juvenilia composed between 1700 and 1710, the span between composition and publication is seventeen years; for 1711 to 1720 it shrinks to only five years, but that is still a considerable amount of time when one remembers the speed with which his translations appeared—the translation of the *Odyssey* apparently was begun a few months after the appearance of the *Iliad* in 1720, and its five volumes were published in 1725–26 (Mack, *Life,* 389)—and the rapidity with which pirated poems were printed, usually a matter of weeks. What was Pope doing with his manuscript texts during the time before they were printed?

This practice of circulating texts in manuscript to multiple readers becomes a challenge for editors dealing with Pope's surviving texts, in particular with his minor pieces. As Ault notes, with the exception of his Homer translations, most of Pope's works in prose and verse were originally published anonymously (*New Light,* 2, 4). The nature of the difficulties faced by an editor attempting to establish a canon and chronology of Pope's shorter works suggests that the manuscripts had a very lively social literary career of their own. "Of [some poems] there are several holographs," Ault notes, "of one ("The Court Ballad") a text must be constructed from an early draft in the poet's hand, a later transcript, and a pirated issue; of another ("Verses on a Grotto") the editor must pick his way through ten contemporary transcripts" (xviii). The existence of multiple fair copies, multiple transcripts by others, and unauthorized print versions suggests that, rather than languishing unread for lack of printer's ink, the poems were instead being circulated for private readers and were participating in the interactive literary mode of additions, adaptations, and responses characteristic of manuscript circulated texts.

Of course, not all of Pope's manuscript pieces that were read and circulated arrived in print. Pope repeatedly refers to his early attempts at writing an epic in his conversations with Joseph Spence. Pope told Spence that he began "Alcander Prince of Rhodes" when he was twelve years old: "I endeavoured, (said he smiling), in this poem, to collect all the beauties of the great epic writers into one piece" (*Anecdotes,* 167). In addition to imitating Milton, Spenser, Cowley, Homer, Virgil, Statius, and Ovid, Pope included in the first book an underwater scene that he apparently remembered with fondness, and he completed four books of about a thousand verses each. Pope kept this juvenilia and apparently let others read it, for he notes twice, "[I had] the copy by me, till I burnt it, by the advice of the Bishop of Rochester"; Pope says elsewhere concerning the manuscript, "I saw his advice was well grounded, and followed it, though not without some regret" (*Anecdotes,* 167, 129).

One can also see more details of the dynamics of manuscript authorship at work in the young poet's career in his relationship with William Wycherley and William Walsh. Wycherley, who was in his sixties when he became acquainted with the teenage Pope, never deliberately printed any of his own verse, engaging instead in social, coterie exchanges. Towards the end of his life, Wycherley decided to send his manuscript poems to the young man with the idea of having them printed together as a volume. Pope, looking back as an older man himself, recalled, "[Wycherley was] really angry with me for correcting his verses so much. I was extremely plagued, up and down, for almost two years with them" (*Anecdotes,* 107). Wycherley did not publish the corrected volume, but it was printed posthumously by Theobald; Pope notes that the verses that are published "are a mixture of Wycherley's own original lines, with a great many of mine inserted here and there, (but not difficult to be distinguished) and some of Wycherley's softened a little in the running, probably by Theobald, who had the chief care of that edition." It is important to note that Pope spent two years involved on a project that would never see print under his name but instead was an activity on his part more typical of social authorship and manuscript culture than an apprenticeship for commercial publication.

With William Walsh, Pope also had the attention of a man at home both in the world of manuscript circulation and in the world of print. Phyllis Freeman characterizes Walsh as *réclame des coteries,* whose literary career consisted more of "the ephemeral exchanges of club and coffeehouse than [of] his slight published work."[17] It is interesting to compare Walsh's entrance into the world of print in comparison with Pope's some two decades later. Walsh's first publication was *A Dialogue Concerning Women, Being a Defense of the Sex* (1691), which was addressed to Walsh's mistress, Eugenia, countess of Kingston. One commentator described this text as "enjoying a well-defined pre-print life."[18] Upon his mistress's remarriage (and not to him), Walsh wrote to Dryden sometime in 1690, sending him the essay along with an "Epigram & an Elegy" for his comments: "at your leisure to look over & tell mee your opinion of it; as also of ye Verses. I see my self 'tis incorrect, but 'twas writt in haste, in obedience to the command of a fair Lady."[19]

Upon receipt of Dryden's favorable view of the piece ("your apostrophe's to your Mistresse, where you break off the thrid [*sic*] of your discourse, and address yourself to her, are, in my opinion, as fine turnes of gallantry, as I have mett with anywhere" [36]), Walsh then broached the topic of publication. His representation of his motives and at the steps through which the manuscript went before arriving in print raise several issues for consideration.

> Wee young Authors are like young Women, who are allways plaguing a Man, when hee is once acquainted wth yr infirmities. I have lookt over my Dialogue of Women, & if I can judge of my own things, as impartially as of other peoples, I think it not much worse yn many other things yt are printed with tolerable Success. However 'tis upon a particular reason yt I would have it printed; of wch I will make you Confident; The Lady to whom it is written has playd mee some scurvy tricks for which I may come to fall out publickly

with her. & because it is usual for all ye Sex to take one anothers part in these case[s]; I wou'd first print this Defence of 'em, to engage my self a party amongst 'em. . . . I have another Mistress, who is resolved to conferr favour upon none but Merit; & as shee is a person of sense, so shee does place all this merit, as Women usually do, in a fine outside; But is a great friend to Witt & Learning; If I coud therefor any ways make her believe yt I had any pretences to those, it might bee a great meens towards ye making mee succeed. The Business therefore is that I have hardly confidence enough in it, to print in my own name; on ye other side shoud it bee printed wthout any name at all, it may perhaps never come to bee read: Now if you woud give your selfe ye trouble to write some little preface to it, it might [sic] a very great means to recommend it to ye World. . . . All yt I would have done in the case, is to acquaint em, yt ye Author of it having not confidence enough in ye piece to venture it to ye press; you thought yt might pass as well as others yt they have been troubled with. If you finde any thing in ye manner, of ye Dialogue, in ye Gallantry of ye Apostrophes, or if you think there is somewhat of reading shewn in it, yt is considerable for a man who professes himself so perfect a servt to ye Sex, you may please to let 'em know as much. (38–39)

As Ward notes, Dryden followed Walsh's suggestions pretty much to the letter in constructing the preface (159 n. 2). Revenge and seduction seem equal and linked motives for appearing in print in Walsh's representation; he also shows a confident knowledge of the formulas of print prefaces. Kraus observes that the ploy appears to have worked: Walsh selectively distributed author's copies of the printed text to ensure that the appropriate parties received his message (as Kraus also points out, Walsh thus parallels the distribution of script texts in coterie practice). Indeed, it did attract the attention of a young lady, Jane Leveson-Gower, who translated the text into French and republished it anonymously and carried on a literary flirtation with Walsh through Dryden.[20] When discussing Pope's love of stratagems and his intricate revenge on Edmund Curll for the printing of *Court Poems,* Walsh's example is a striking precedent.

In addition to this publication and *Letters and Poems Amorous and Gallant* (1692), Walsh left behind two collections of verse and epistles and a collection of letters and prose pieces.[21] He thus created a comparable body of print and script texts. The apparent copy text for the printer for *Letters and Poems* includes seven unpublished poems, which Freeman notes are "crossed [out] lightly, perhaps for the publisher's information" ("Walsh

Manuscripts," 397 n. 3). In his later relationship with Pope, Walsh appears to have acted primarily as a critical reader for the young poet, encouraging and correcting manuscripts Pope shared with him. Pope declared to Spence that he met Walsh in 1705 and shortly thereafter showed him the "Essay on Criticism" (*Anecdotes,* 127); in another place he dates their meeting earlier, occurring when Pope was around fifteen. "He used to encourage me much," Pope told Spence, "and used to tell me, that there was one way left of excelling: for though we had several great poets, we never had any one great poet that was correct; and he desired me to make that my study and aim" (*Anecdotes,* 169). Pope mentioned as well that Walsh read his early translation of Statius, which was afterwards printed integrating Walsh's corrections (168).

Pope's manuscript exchanges with other literary individuals also confirm our sense of the continuation of social, manuscript literary culture simultaneously with the world of commercial translation. Pope's friendship with the man about town, Henry Cromwell, gives the lie to Pope's poetic protestation "I ne'er with Wits or Witlings past my days / To spread the Itch of Verse and Praise." Cromwell occasionally printed pieces in miscellanies, but he is firmly of the world of social, "holiday" poets who took little interest in publication. Unlike Wycherley, Cromwell's verse exchanges with Pope show both men more interested in a pleasurable display of their talents than polishing working drafts for the printer.

Nearly every letter to Cromwell in the years 1707–10 contains references to Cromwell's reading of Pope's works and his receipt of Cromwell's. When sending him his "Ode to Solitude," Pope queries Cromwell, "[Would you] oblige me with the Trust of any Thing of yours?" (*Correspondence,* 1:68). Concerning Cromwell's writings, Pope urged in 1710,

> Let us communicate our Works for our mutual Comfort; se[nd] me Elegies, and you shall not want Heroics. As present I only have these Arguments in Prose to the Thebaid, which you claim by Promise, as I do your Translation of —*Pars me Suylmo tenet*—and the Ring. The rest I hope for as soon as you can conveniently transcribe 'em. (1:81–82)

In another letter to Cromwell he offers a mock apology for imposing on Cromwell with his own verses: "I hope, you think me none of those / Who shew their Parts as *Pentlow* does, / I lug out to one or two / Such Friends, if such there are, as you" (1:29). These letters also reveal that Sherburn was deceived in believing that Pope exercised little control over his manuscript copies until being stung by Curll's piracies in 1716. As early as 1707 one finds him writing to both Cromwell and Wycherley, "I beg the favour of You to Let [the poems] go no farther than your Chamber," stating elsewhere, "I desire you will be so kind to me as not to show what I send to anybody" (1:31, 36, 58). Although some of his verses addressed particularly to Cromwell were later printed ("An Epistle to H. Cromwell," 1707, printed 1727; "Letter to Cromwell," 1708, printed 1727), it is clear from the context of the correspondence, which was the means of conveying and transmitting the texts, that Pope was not primarily concerned with building a reputation based on the commercial presentation of these particular texts.

As we have seen, Cromwell was not the only individual with whom Pope was engaged in epistolary exchange, but through him Pope was also affiliated with a larger manuscript circulation network, as revealed in comments in his letters about the manuscripts of third parties in Cromwell's possession. Cromwell was obviously reading and circulating many more writers' manuscripts than Pope's: Pope in one letter requests a copy of one of Gay's poems, for example (1:25). It was, of course, through the poet Elizabeth Thomas, the lover of Henry Cromwell and a correspondent with John Dryden, Mary Chudleigh, Mary Astell, and John Norris, that Pope's letters eventually ended up in Edmund Curll's hands.

Although their relationship falls outside the time frame for this investigation of Pope's early career, it is worth noting briefly some of the similarities concerning manuscript texts that occur in Pope's correspondence with Lady Mary Wortley Montagu. During the period in which they were friends, the evidence is clear that they exchanged verse manuscripts freely. Lady Mary, for example, had in her possession a copy of "The Universal Prayer," which long predated its publication (Sherburn, 145–50). Pope's letters to her in 1717 reveal that he had read and transcribed in fair copy many of her verses, including the "Court Poems" and her "Pastorals," swearing that he had kept them "locked up and concealed from all prophane eyes" (*Correspondence*, 1:441 n). He sent her unidentified short pieces, and she sent him translations from the Turkish.[22] Lady Mary sent transcriptions of his verse to her friends in the 1720s, urging, "I beg they may dye . . . and never go farther than your Closet" (*Complete Letters*, 2:15) To Lady Mar she sent a copy of Pope's response to Gay's poem congratulating Pope on finishing his house; Pope, meanwhile, was sending his own copies of it to Judith Cowper. In this example we can see the ripple effect of social authorship through manuscript circulation.

It was Lady Mary's *Court Poems,* of course, that led to the first of the famous quarrels with Curll. In effect, the publication history of this text exemplifies both the practices of coterie or social authorship and the hazards of the transition to the printed page. In "The Politics of Female Authorship: Lady Mary Wortley Montagu's Reaction to the Printing of Her Poems," Isobel Grundy observes that in the stormy career of Lady Mary Wortley Montagu the ambition of authorship played a large but mostly secret part.[23] The attribution of the three eclogues making up the *Court Poems* has served as a matter for debate, being variously assigned to Pope, Gay, and Lady Mary and in varying proportions; what is clear is that an individual named Joseph Jacobs gave to John Oldmixon "three poems at that time handed about, entitled 'The Basset Table,' 'The Toilet' and the 'Drawing Room,'" as being by Lady Mary, who in turn showed them to Curll.[24] Despite Pope's attempt to convince Curll not to publish, Curll did so, and there was apparently a floodgate of gossip concerning who the authors were, aggravated in part by the declaration on the preface that the text was "Published faithfully, as they were found in a Pocket-Book taken up in Westminister-Hall, the last Day of the Lord Winton's Tryal," which, as Curll's biographer notes, was a sensational case of high treason (Straus, 52). According to Curll, Pope had Bernard Lintot introduce them socially; Pope supposedly observed to Curll, "*Satire* should not be printed. . . . I [Curll] answered They should not be wrote, for if they were they would be printed. He replied, Mr. Gay's Interest at Court would be greatly hurt by publishing these *Poems,*" and then Pope apparently proceeded to slip a strong emetic into Curll's wine (Straus, 52). Pope wrote to Caryll explaining that he was involved in a "most ridiculous quarrel with a bookseller": "[It was] occasioned by his having printed some satirical pieces on the Court under my name. I contrived to save the fellow a beating by giving him a vomit."[25]

There is little in Pope's early correspondence or in his later observations to Joseph Spence that supports an image of him as primarily concerned with a print market for his occasional verse, which his subsequent critics appear to believe he harbored from his first visit to Will's Coffee House. Indeed, if friends who bombard one with manuscripts can be a nuisance, as he suggests to Cromwell, worse yet in Pope's opinion are those whom he satirizes in a letter to him written in 1708.

'Tis a Mercy I do not assault you with a number of Original Sonnets & Epigrams, which our modern Bards put forth in the Spring time in as great abundance, as Trees do Blossoms, a very few of whereof ever come to Fruit, & please no longer than just in their Birth. So that they make no less haste to bring [the]ir Flow'rs of Wit to the Press, than Gardners to bring their other flow'rs to the [m]arket. . . . Tis the happiness of the Age, that the Modern Invention of printing Poems for a Pence a piece has brought the Nosegays of Parnassus to bear the same Price. (*Correspondence,* 1:56)

As David Foxon chronicled, it was Pope's contract with Lintot for a subscription edition of the *Iliad* that made Pope financially independent, not the occasional verse.[26] Pope told Spence that he believed that Dryden had cleared "about twelve hundred pounds by his Virgil; and had sixpence each line for his Fables" (*Anecdotes,* 160). In contrast, Pope received £200 for each volume of the *Iliad* in addition to all the copies for his subscribers and presentation copies: Spence estimated the overall value to Pope as nearly £6,000, while Foxon more cautiously suggests a more modest £5,000, but it is still a phenomenal figure for a literary property at the time (*Anecdotes,* 176 n; Foxon, 63).

One can compare these figures with the amounts Pope received for selling the copyright on pieces that circulated in manuscript for five or more years. Lintot paid £15 for the copyright for "An Essay on Criticism" in 1716, five years after its initial appearance in 1711; Pope received £26 19s. for his contributions to Lintot's *Miscellany* between 1712 and 1726–27 (one of only two paid by Lintot); *The Rape of the Lock* secured £15.[27] To rephrase Dr. Johnson, while it maybe true that none but blockheads write except for money, compared with what could be earned with editions and translations, Pope would have had to have been a blockhead to consider his occasional verse as an important and reliable source of income. His commentators, however, persist in grouping all of his literary output under the commercial, moneymaking label, regardless of whether they made him much money at all.

Thus, the question arises, in his treatment of his editions and his occasional verse, did Pope manifest any differences in the way in which he handled the manuscript text before and after publication? Again, one must rely on incomplete sightings of manuscript texts as they were conveyed from reader to reader in correspondence and also on the existence of his manuscript readers' copies of such texts. In his analysis of the Caryll family papers, Howard Erskine-Hill discovered a manuscript volume of sixteenth-, seventeenth-, and eighteenth-century verse that contains versions of three of Pope's poems, "Upon Silence" (published in 1712 as "On Silence"), "on some flowers in silk wrought by a handsome young lady," and "the River," which he dates as being copied in 1703 ("Pope at Fifteen," 268, 273). As Erskine-Hill points out, there exists another manuscript copy of "On Silence," which Butt dated as about 1702. Butt points out that, in general, there is "considerable difference between the manuscripts of the early and the manuscripts of the later poems. Of the early poems no rough draft is extant. Each survives only in a fair copy made to permit the poem to be submitted to friends for advance, or when it was preparing for press" (548).

As we can see in the case of the Caryll manuscript volume, some survived in more than one copy. Butt describes how the 1712 printed version of "On Silence" differs from the manuscript text, using only seventeen of the first forty-eight lines; Butt believes that the changes are the result of a twenty-four-year-old poet's improved versification. "The River" was printed fourteen years later, with only four of the ten stanzas found in the Caryll manuscript (275); in contrast to Butt's explanation for the omissions in "On Silence," Erskine-Hill notes that the 1703 version was "a piece of precocious love-poetry with a more consistent and extensive design than appears in the printed version" (276). Interestingly, Erskine-Hill notes that "it is hard to say why Pope rejected these stanzas; it may be relevant that they are somewhat nearer the bone, less lightly fanciful, than his other protestations of love in the imitations of Waller and Cowley, the group of poems to which 'The River' belongs." What this group of early manuscripts suggests is that Pope perhaps had more than one motive to have more than one version of his occasional verse.

Erskine-Hill does not speculate in whose hand these early texts are, except that it is not Pope's, so we are not sure whether it is Caryll's or that of a member of his family. John Caryll, whom Sherburn describes as a "person of no interest to the public," has chiefly been of interest to Pope's critics and biographers as the person who requested Pope to write "The Rape of the Lock" and as the source of the doctored letters, which Pope originally wrote to him but then later revised and published as his correspondence with Addison and Wycherley (Sherburn, 20–21). Mack likewise focuses on Caryll as the recipient of Pope's letters, noting only that Caryll had keen literary interests and a literary acquaintance that included at various times Dryden, Wycherley, and the actor Thomas Betterton (*Life*, 89). What the manuscript volume of verse suggests, however, is that Caryll or some member of his family was also participating with Pope in manuscript exchanges in the early years of 1700 in the same fashion as we saw other Catholic provincial families such as the Astons and the Carys earlier in the 1650s.[28]

If we wish to see a later example of Pope's practice of reshaping into longer printed pieces his early manuscript materials that had enjoyed previous circulation separately in his correspondence, Butt offers us tantalizing glimpses in his account of the manuscripts involved with Pope's 1735 "Epistle to Dr. Arbuthnot." Butt describes the manuscript at the Pierpont Morgan Library, New York, as a "teasing collection of fragments," the largest of which is 260 lines (553). Pope himself described the text to Arbuthnot, in a letter dated August 1734, as having been written "by piecemeal many years, & wch I have now made haste to put together" (quoted in Butt, 560), which is echoed by his opening of the "Advertisement": "This Paper is a Sort of Bill of Complaint, begun many years since, and drawn up by snatches, as the several Occasions offer'd." The opening of this manuscript, which has been canceled, is markedly different from the printed version:

> And of myself too something must I say?
> Take then this Verse, the Trifle of a Day;
> And if it lives, it lives but to commend,
> The Man of Friendship, but no boasting Friend,
> The Man of Courage, but not prone to fight,
> The Man of Learning, yet too wise to write.
>
> (in Butt, 554)

Butt goes on to speculate that these original opening lines describe not Arbuthnot but instead Major Cleland, who is believed to have lent his name to the "Letter to the Publisher" prefacing *The Dunciad* and a 1731 letter to the *Daily Post Boy* defending Pope's "Epistle to Burlington" (555–56). Butt argues that the draft was composed early in 1732; the Pierpont manuscript lacks several significant characters and scenes from the final version, including the portraits of Sapho and Sporus and the poet's aging parents. Butt explains that "those beautiful lines describing the poet at his mother's deathbed were in existence in September 1731, for in that month Pope sent a copy of them in a letter to Aaron Hill" (560), which lends credence to Pope's observation of the piecemeal composition of the whole and establishes the independent existence of parts of the texts as manuscript pieces.

The teasing nature of the early manuscript and the assorted fragments is amplified for modern critics and bibliographers because, as suggested before, we are more accustomed to think of a long poem as being composed as unified, organic whole, perhaps over a lengthy period of time but nevertheless having a structural integrity. Pope's practice of writing what we term fragments, which circulated independently, sometimes for several years, before being combined and reshaped into a longer work—as in the case of "Windsor-Forest" and "Epistle to Dr. Arbuthnot"—runs contrary to a modern definition of a poem as a unified object of composition but is quite consistent with the dynamics of social, manuscript texts, constantly open to alteration and adaptation for new readers and new contexts.

We know about the extent of the manuscript circulation of some of Pope's poems, however, because of the ingenuity of the booksellers in getting hold of them for print after Pope's translations increased his market value. Lintot took the direct approach after the appearance of *The Pastorals,* advertising in October 1711 in the *General Post* seeking "excellent Copies by Pope, Butler, and Mr. Smith for inclusion in a planned miscellany" (Ault, *New Light,* 137–38). In his dedication to the 1714 version of "The Rape of the Lock," Pope reveals a reason for the double publication: "An imperfect copy having been offer'd to a Bookseller, you had the Good-nature for my Sake to consent to the Publication of one more correct: This I was forc'd to before I had executed half of my Design, for the Machinery was entirely wanting to compleat it."[29] Although Sherburn maintains that Curll's appropriation of "The First Psalm" and "The Court Poems" in 1716 effectively checked Pope's practice of showing his verses in manuscript, as we have seen in the example of "The Epistle to Dr. Arbuthnot," this was clearly not the case (Sherburn, 183–84).

Many of these short pieces that ended up in print anonymously in miscellanies or newspapers such as the *St. James Chronicle* or the *Weekly Packet* were originally written in letters or formed parts of a verse exchange. Swift sardonically described how a hack writer could make use of Pope's habits of reading and writing: "Ye Poets ragged and forlorn, / Down from your garrets haste," he opens—

I know a trick to make you thrive;
　O, 'tis a quaint device:
Your still-born poems shall revive,
　And scorn to wrap up spice

Get all your verse printed fair,
　Then let them well be dried;
And Curll must have a special care
　To leave the margin wide.

Lend these to paper-sparing Pope;
　And when he sets to write,
No letter with an envelope,
　Could give him more delight.

When Pope has fill'd the margins round,
　Why then recall your loan;
Sell them to Curll for fifty pound,
　And swear they are your own.

(Quoted in Straus, 49)

As ridiculous as Swift's scheme may seem, Pope did apparently mingle his verses with those sent to him. There is, for example, the countess of Winchilsea's poem, "To Mr. Pope, in Answer to a Copy of Verses," a piece clearly designed to participate in a social culture of manuscript authorship rather than print, from its title to its fate serving as scratch paper on which Pope roughed out book 13 of the *Iliad*. Her verse was printed in 1717, only a few years after the *Iliad's* publication, but Pope's poem to her that apparently began the exchange, "Impromptu to Lady Winchilsea," Ault dates as before 1714; Ault notes that although contemporary transcripts existed, it was not printed until 1741 (120–21). Cromwell, Caryll, Aaron Hill, and the Blount sisters all received numerous small poems as parts of letters or as complete verse epistles; many of these ended up as anonymous publications, some never formally acknowledged by Pope after they had been printed.[30] One example would be "A Hym to Windsor-Forest," written in 1717 to the Blount sisters, which did not appear in print until 1831.

For a more extended example that illustrates the process by which Pope's occasional verses circulated, we can examine the journal and scrapbook of

Mrs. Charles Caesar. Mrs. Caesar has typically figured in Pope studies for her contribution to his subscription of the *Odyssey,* for which Pope dubbed her *Processit Caesaris astrum.*[31] However, as her manuscript journal reveals, in addition to her political interests and her ability to be a literary fundraiser, Mrs. Caesar was a keen reader of material sent to her by Pope, both his and by others, and herself an occasional verse writer. She records, "The Duke of Wharton's speech against Bolingbroke he [Pope] gave me the Morning he left England, desireing I would Not give a Coppy, Many Great have read, and all admir, and I value as a sort of Legacy, Not being of Pops [*sic*] Mind, that he Wanted an Honest Heart" (Erskine-Hill, "Caesar," 441). In her journal, she also includes couplets about Bathurst, annotating them "Pope rote thus," which Erskine-Hill states are an addition to Pope's canon.

In a more extended example of her exchanges with Pope, she notes cryptically, "Missing a line I had [quoted], Pope looking Mist the Poim [*sic*], sent it with These [lines] (I saying how shall I contrive room for all your Works)" (443). The short six-line poem appears in the Twickenham edition as "Lines to King George II," but it is taken from a contemporary transcript in the Portland Papers, endorsed in Lord Oxford's hand (443). Erskine-Hill explains the scrambled lineage of this particular manuscript text as follows:

> Mrs. Caesar quotes [in a letter] to Pope a line of his verse but cannot find it in her copies of his poems. Pope concludes that she has not got or has mislaid the poem from which it comes. He promises to send it to her. . . . When Pope sends the poem he encloses with it the couplet beginning: "O all-accomplished Caesar" and humorously alludes to his own small size. The remaining verses are then written as a reply to Pope's compliment ("'tis true Great Bard . . . ") and are conceivably of Mrs. Caesar's own composing, though more likely she went to her husband for help. . . . The two parts of the joint poem were no doubt then shown to Oxford, whom the Caesars visited. This reconstruction is confirmed by Mrs. Caesar's scrapbook itself. . . . The first two lines are in Pope's hand (a fragment of paper stuck in the book) while the final four are in Mrs. Caesar's, prefaced by her note: 'To Mr Pope from me.' (443–44)[32]

Whether or not one agrees with Erskine-Hill that Mrs. Caesar had to seek out her husband's help to create the verses, it is a clear example of the type of manuscript circulation—both the reading and writing of—that flourished in the seventeenth century, even to the confusion of the individual attributions and the multiple versions.

If one denies Pope's investment in manuscript culture that we have seen, there are numerous oddities about his authorial practices considered only from a modern commercial viewpoint. Butt commented on the care with which Pope preserved his early fair copies, attributing it to "sentimental reasons" (552). Another possible explanation, however, which takes into consideration Pope's involvement with the manuscript culture of social authorship, might be that Pope kept them in the same fashion that one keeps the first editions of one's printed texts after newer ones are issued—they are the first version but never the final one, the ever dynamic material alive and available for transformation at the author's desire. It would also be the case that, unlike the way in which we gleefully throw out the typescript of our book after the print galleys have been safely corrected, Pope and his friends clearly had no difficulty reading and enjoying texts in script form as well as print. Pope's adherence to the practices of manuscript circulation may explain in part the degree to which he felt free to alter, combine, and expand his verses throughout his career, creating multiple versions of major pieces and combining and recombining shorter pieces to create larger ones.

If one looks at Pope's close friends and readers during the early years, another reason for his continued participation in the older practices of manuscript authorship emerges clearly. Of the friends mentioned so far as recipients of Pope's manuscripts, it is interesting to note the number of them who also wrote for a manuscript readership. While Walsh, Congreve, Garth, Bolingbroke, and Swift were writing for both publication and private exchange, Horace Walpole's catalogue of noble authors has several entries that overlap with the original readership of *The Pastorals* before publication: of those listed by Pope as having read that manuscript, Granville, Garth, Talbot, Somers, and the bishop of Rochester were poets whose public reputations as writers were based on private manuscript circulation. Sherburn again comments on the seeming oddity of Pope's extensive literary acquaintances while at Binfield in Berkshire: "In this retired spot he acquired a circle of friends both numerous and distinguished. From the extreme of obscurity he arrived at the pinnacle of fame in less than a decade, and his friends as well as his genius aided this success" (45). It was the practice of circulating manuscript pieces and of reading others' manuscript texts, however, that gained him this influential circle even though he himself was isolated in the countryside.

For a final comparison of Pope's practice of authorship in the context of competing manuscript and print cultures, it is illuminating to consider the career of a poet Pope caused to have printed in the 1717 *Miscellany* but whom critics without fail ignore in connections with Pope and his publication practices. Elizabeth Singer Rowe enjoyed considerable reputation as the "Pindaric Lady," although she objected strongly to printing her poems. Born fourteen years before Pope in 1674, Elizabeth Singer also attracted attention for her verses while still young, a "little copy of verses of hers securing the admiration of Lord Weymouth in 1694. Her fame spread with her paraphrases of Job written at the request of Bishop Kenn, but not printed."[33] John Dunton printed short pieces by her anonymously after the turn of the century; it was Dunton who gave her the name the "Pindaric Lady." But even so, her biographer declares, she "could not be perswaded to publish her works by subscription or even to accept the advantageous terms offered by the booksellers, if she would permit her scattered pieces to be collected and published together" (242). She stoutly resisted publication for her poetry because "she wrote verse through inclination, and rather as an amusement, than as a study and profession, to excel in which she should make the business of her life" (229). Such a position concerning print authorship matches exactly with the views expressed by the manuscript authors discussed in the first essay, both male and female, aristocratic and middle class.

One can also compare Elizabeth Singer Rowe's statement about manuscript versus print authorship with Pope's explanation in his preface to *The Works* printed in 1717: "It was want of consideration that made me an author; I writ because it amused me; I corrected because it was as pleasant to me to correct as to write; and I publish'd because I was told I might please such as it was a credit to please" (*Prose*, 1:292). While twentieth-century commentators find such declarations by Pope laughable, or duplicitous, when it is placed not against the culture of commercial print practices but in the context of coterie authorship, it is clearly in the spirit and terms used by Pope's own literary contemporaries who continued to participate in manuscript culture.

This is not to suggest that Pope was oblivious to the perils of remaining within the manuscript culture and the mentality that could accompany it. In addition to his remark about holiday poets, in the 1713 *Guardian* essay "On Easy Writing," Pope pokes gentle fun at two young ladies using the names Astrea and Dorinda, "exchanging verses of Love and Friendship," those immortal themes of coterie poets (*Prose,* 1:93). In the preface to *The Works,* Pope ironically points out that one reason poets are driven to seek publication is because of the limits of their manuscript readership to evaluate honestly the poet's productions: "their particular friends may be either ignorant, or insincere; and the rest of the world too well bred to shock them with a truth, which generally their Booksellers are the first that inform them of" (*Prose,* 1:290). Clearly, however, for Pope the benefits of continuing his participation in the exchange of manuscripts, the creation of interactive, dynamic texts involving his friends, overrode the need to control absolutely access to his works, as critics such as Butt, Sherburn, and Mack have believed.

Pope's continued allegiance to the practices of manuscript culture are part of the reason, I believe, why his life and literary career are dotted with oddities when viewed purely through the lens of commercial print publication. None of the information about the existence of Pope's manuscripts or literary friends who exchanged verses with him and who provided the initial audience for his occasional verse is new. When this diverse group of literary acquaintances—the Carylls, the Blounts, William Walsh, the bishop of Rochester, the countess of Winchilsea, Aaron Hill, Mrs. Caesar—is included equally in our assessment of Pope's practices of authorship along with Addison, Swift, and Gay, and the booksellers, it seems clear that Pope's original commitment to the world of manuscript culture continued and nourished his participation in the world of print. Pope's readers would have had the pleasure of reading his verse repeatedly through the years, first in script and then in print, first as part of a social practice of reading and writing and then as part of a commercial world of satire and commentary.

FOUR

Getting into Print

London and the
Social Author

An heavenly Afflatus causes me sometimes to fall into Tears of Joy, assured, that the Lord has heard my Supplications about this matter [finding a London publisher for "Magnalia"]. And now, its having been thus delayed, and obstructed and clogg'd, proves but an opportunity for that Prayer and Faith, and for those Experiences, which if I had gone without, the Publication of that Book, would not have proved near so sweet a mercy to me. But, if it should miscarry, after all, O my God, my God what Confusion would ensue upon me!
Cotton Mather, *Diary*

In the first two essays, we encountered authors who never published and never desired to and authors who were published against their will. Several of the authors discussed as social, manuscript authors did have their works printed after their death, either by family members or by later generations of literary editors recovering seventeenth-century verse. This essay is devoted to the writer who, having initially participated in a social, manuscript literary culture, decided to see his or her texts in print but did not derive significant income from publishing or literary activities or expect to do so as a result of publication. What was the experience of getting into print for this category of author, prose as well as poetry, before the passage of the Act of Queen Anne in 1709? What practical details were involved in print authorship in comparison with manuscript? What was required on the part of authors to ensure that their text was printed as they desired? In this essay we shall focus on authors who worked with printers in London and in the subsequent essay on those authors writing and publishing in provincial English presses as well as in Scotland and Wales.

As opposed to script authorship (which required only a pen and paper and the author him- or herself), getting into print in the seventeenth and early eighteenth centuries for the majority of writers who deliberately sought out the new mode of authorship still involved lengthy negotiations by the author with several different individual technicians at different stages of production.[1] In addition, despite our perception of a boom or a surge in print texts, the business of publishing was still highly centralized in terms of its availability and was legally restricted in terms of numbers of presses available to provide services to authors.

In 1615, the Court of Stationers Company had ordered that only twenty-two printers be permitted to work in London; by 1660, Sir Roger L'Estrange estimated that there were sixty printers in London, but he also strongly recommended that they be reduced to twenty.[2] His advice was followed in the Licensing Act of 1662, whereby, in order to lessen the numbers of available printers, it was mandated that no more new master printers be approved until the number had been reduced to twenty (Plant, 83–84). As we shall see in next essay, authors in the provinces who would not—or could not—travel to London faced limited options. For example, in Scotland between 1671 and 1680, printing was legally restricted by patent to a single royal printer; in Ireland, as Pollard's study describes, "from 1551 when the first book was printed in Ireland to 1680, no more than one printer was at work in Dublin at any one time," because of this same practice, the monopoly of the king's printer.[3] The three provincial presses in Ireland that had sprung up during the Commonwealth were closed, and rival Dublin presses that attempted to challenge the patent were put out of business.

Even though Julie Stone Peters' study of Congreve and the press asserts as a premise that, "by the Restoration, 'every person of breeding' had easy access to books, if not a complete and well-documented library . . . and reading in the provinces . . . spread with the founding of provincial printing and publishing after 1695" (15), when one looks at the actual numbers of presses and printers involved in this "spread" of print, the numbers are surprisingly low and localized. As late as 1724, in all of the kingdom, there were only twenty-eight printing houses in the provinces—not a very encompassing spread—and although London boasted seventy-five, most operated only a single printing press. As John Feather observed in his study of the provincial book trade in the eighteenth century, "in 1695, there was not tradition of provincial printing,"[4] and even after the lapse of the licensing act, London booksellers and printers successfully controlled copyrights and distribution. In Feather's opinion, "London remained the only significant centre of English publishing" (4). As the historian of the print trade Marjorie Plant observed of the preceding generation, "it seems almost incredible that our Elizabethan and early Stuart literature should have issued from between 50 & 60 [individual machines], a number, of course, exceeded in many a single printing establishment today" (87); as bibliographers and historians of print have known, but literary critics apparently have not, these numbers were not dramatically different in the 1670s and 1690s.

But let us say that our author, undaunted by the small numbers of printers available and his or her distance from London, was still determined to go into print, although not anticipating much financial return or reward; what type of negotiations took place in order to become a print author? Obviously, the most desirable scenario for our author was to be solicited by a bookseller or publisher for his or her writings, as we have seen in the case of Pope and Elizabeth Singer Rowe. Booksellers also advertised for manuscripts: as we saw in the previous essay, in order to prepare an edition, Lintot advertised for good copies of Pope's and Swift's texts, and Edmund Curll was a ready market for any writer whose reputation was already established.

From the 1690s on, periodicals were promising venues for writers who were in search of a publisher for short pieces—such as single poems, essays, and epistles—but were expecting little or no payment. In addition to literary venues and news gazettes, publications such as the *Philosophical Transactions* of the Royal Society published letters and short accounts of natural phenomena and experiments conducted not only by those attending the meetings in London but also by correspondents in the provinces and New England. While Richard Waller was secretary and overseeing the production of the *Transactions* from 1691 to 1693, he would often request materials from amateur scientists who communicated with the Royal Society. For example, he wrote to Sir Robert Sibbold in Edinburgh thanking him for sending a treatise about whales cast up on shore and asking, "If you have any Small Tracts by you that are too little to be publisht by themselves, if you permit their Insertions in the Philosophical Transactions, . . . such papers will be preserved that might otherwise be lost."[5] In a similar vein, Waller wrote to Hans Sloane, reminding him, "You were pleased to give me hopes of a Paper Concerning ye Earthquake in the Western Parts of ye

World which I intreat you not to forget but at your leisure to draw up for ye Press."[6] In addition to such invitations from Waller, the letterbooks of the Royal Society contain numerous other examples of this type of correspondence from the compilers of the *Philosophical Transactions* seeking materials from members and readers.

Literary periodicals such as the *Gentleman's Journal,* published briefly in 1691–92, also urged readers to submit their short pieces—and even those by their friends—by leaving them at a coffeehouse and then reading about their acceptance or rejection in a future issue.[7] This practice of encouraging readers' participation was also used by Dunton's *Athenian Gazette* and *Athenian Mercury,* which urged readers to send responses to letters, poems, and riddles. Both professional hack and amateur writers responded, some more famous than others, including a "Mr. Swift" (whom Dunton's footnote identifies as "afterwards the celebrated Dean of St. Patricks"): "[a] Country Gentleman sent an Ode to the Athenian Society; which, being an ingenious Poem, was prefixed to the Fifth Supplement of the Athenian Mercury" (Dunton, 1:193). Indeed, Dunton says that the response from readers was so great that "we were immediately overloaded with Letters. . . . Sometimes I have found several hundreds for me at Mr. Smith's Coffee-house in Stocks Market, where we usually met to consult matters" (1:189).

But of course, in order to participate in the periodicals' projects, whether scientific observations or literary games and riddles, one had to be able to purchase or have access to the print publications. Next, one would have to arrange to have one's response conveyed to whatever London coffeehouse served as the editor's office, perhaps by the new Penny Post, with which Dunton denied he was in league to boost its business.

If one's manuscript was a pamphlet or book-length volume, one's practical problems as an author were increased. The Welsh prophet Arise Evans informs his "Courteous Reader": "These things have been under a Bushel these nine months so that I was in travaile until now as you see my condition."[8] Evans felt compelled to print his views on the state of the Commonwealth but had no success in finding a printer: "I complained unto many, but I found no assistance, how I might set forth this light to all that are in the house; and especially to them that are in the house of Parliament, and to print it, that it might no longer lye upon my conscience, as a heavie burthern." His solution, as we shall see also in the later example of Cotton Mather, was to involve a higher authority in the publishing business: "at last being over-whelmed with sorrow, I made my complaint unto God, who in an extraordinary manner, within 24 houres did send me help," although Evans ended up having the text published for himself at his own expense (Sig. A2r).

Numerous letters and memoirs from the late seventeenth and early eighteenth centuries demonstrate that getting a book or volume into print often involved physically traveling to London in order to meet the printer or bookseller in person; lovers of the novel will remember *Joseph Andrews,* of course, with Parson Adams' expedition to London with his sermons in his saddlebags, hoping to find a printer for them. The bookseller John Dunton's lively memoirs, *The Life and Errors of John Dunton,* are filled with personal accounts of authors he dealt with in the 1690s, when authors, academic and poetical, would bring their works to his shop for his perusal.

If the author did not travel to London in person, we also find numerous accounts of manuscripts being conveyed to the bookseller by an interested third party. John Dryden, for example, carried Mary, Lady Chudleigh's poems in his coat pocket from rural Devon to London, where he showed them to his own printer, Jacob Tonson. The young Alexander Pope at Binfield in Berkshire, as we have seen, had his pastorals introduced to Tonson in London by a mutual friend, who had the piece in script copy.

Unlike today, as we e-mail journals to ask about submission policies and send abstracts to virtual conferences (or even like Charlotte Brontë's famous boomerang manuscript bundle containing *The Professor,* which supposedly was mailed and remailed in the same wrapper to numerous publishers before being accepted), during the late seventeenth and early eighteenth centuries, the negotiations between author and the purveyors of print technology tended to be one-on-one, individual, personal, and time-consuming, especially if it was a book-length project and if money was involved. If our author was a poet, the negotiations could be even more difficult. As John Dunton bluntly observed, there was no real market for the Muses: "alas! after all, when I see an ingenious man set up for a mere Poet, and steer his course through life towards that Point of the compass, I give him up, as one pricked down by Fate for misery and misfortune. It is something unaccountable," Dunton concluded sadly, "but one would incline to think there is some indispensable Law, whereby Poverty and Disappointment are entailed upon Poets" (1:183).

Students of Restoration literature are familiar with the amounts paid to Milton for *Paradise Lost*—Milton received five pounds down, and five pounds for each edition that sold out. After Milton's death, his widow sold the full copyright to Samuel Simmons for eight pounds (Plant, 74). Poets who were dependent on their writing for a living fared little better. Aphra Behn attempted to get five more pounds out of Jacob Tonson for *Poems Upon Several Occasions* (1684), protesting, "I shou'd really have thought 'em worth thirty pounds; and I hope will find it worth £25." She continues persuasively,

> You can not think wt a preety thinge ye Island will be and wt a deal of labor I shall have yet with it: and if that pleases, I will do the 2d voyage, wch will compose a little book as big as a novel by it self. But pray speake to yor brother to advance the price to one 5 lb more. . . . I vow I wou'd not aske it if I did not really believe it worth more.[9]

Academic translators were often paid only with extra copies of their own books. Dryden was an exception, and his letters show that he repeatedly had difficulties with financial arrangements, even though he remained with one printer, Jacob Tonson, for almost his entire literary career.[10] One of the most famous of these negotiations involved Tonson's counting the lines of translation that Dryden submitted before paying him: Dryden sent only 1,146 lines of Ovid, which caused Tonson politely to protest, "You cannot imagine I expected soe little; for you were pleased to use me much kindlyer in Juvenall [2,280 lines] wch is not reckon'd soe easy to translate as Ovid" (Dryden, *Letters,* 50–52). Dryden dutifully sent more lines.

Once the printer or bookseller agreed to take on a long project, as Marjorie Plant observed, "the person who was no account whatever in the early years of the book industry was the author," since manuscripts were sold outright as property, with the modern concept of author's copyright not coming into law until the Act of Queen Anne in 1709 and not resolved until the late 1770s.[11] Dunton summarizes the pragmatics of publication for the majority of Restoration poets in his gloomy forecast for their financial futures cited earlier, which he concludes by essentially implying that print and poetry were incompatible and, furthermore, "I would not allege all this to dissuade any noble Genius to pursue this Art as a little pretty Divertisement; but where it is made the very Trade of life, I am pretty positive the man is in the wrong box" (1:184). Such a view is in direct contrast to the culture of manuscript authorship: as Marie Burghope observed, for the script author, poetry could be both one's recreation and one's business, whereas in print culture, poetry was a vocational error, equivalent, one might say, of an untenured faculty member writing reviews in unrefereed journals—nice fun, but it won't get you anywhere.

The type of authorship that could make money during the Restoration, the writers that the professionals in the trade themselves considered to be print authors, is a type (like the amateur, social, manuscript author) in which we, as literary historians, have not taken much interest. These are the flocks of what Dunton termed the "Hackney Authors," writers who often lived on the printer's or bookseller's premises, producing text on demand.[12] These authors were engaged in translation, abridgments, and adaptations, and Dunton warns that "these Gormandizers will eat you the very life out of Copy so soon as ever it appears; for, as the times go, Original and Abridgment are almost reckoned as necessary as Man and Wife" (1:52). Dunton deplores the practice of hiring Hacks to produce spin-offs as "a learned kind of theft" (the pirate appears on the horizon again) and a "scandal to the trade," but it is also clear that he himself employed several. He cites a Mr. Ridpath, "a considerable Scholar, and well acquainted with the Languages. He is a Scotsman, and designed first of all for the Ministry; but, some unfortunate accident or other, the fate of an Author came upon him" (1:181). A Mr. Philips likewise earns Dunton's praise, as a "gentleman of good learning, and well born. He will write you a design off in a very little time, if the gout or claret, do not stop him" (1:181). More problematic for success in the print trade are authors such as Mr. Bradshaw. Dunton calls him "the best accomplished hackney-author" he ever met, capable of producing texts in a wide variety of fields but not entirely reliable: "I had once fixed him upon a very great design, and furnished him both with money and books, which were most of them Historical and Geographical; but my Gentleman thought fit to remove himself, and I am not sure that I have seen him since" (1:182).

Once our author, amateur or struggling hack, having traveled to London, secured a printer or bookseller and sold his or her rights in the book-length volume, the real work of print production would begin. Most printers relied on the authors to read proof, for example, requiring either another journey to London or expensive carriage back and forth of texts, or at worst an unchecked text filled with errors: when Mather's *Magnalia* finally was printed in 1702, it contained approximately three hundred errors.[13] John Salusbury, the printer of Robert Fleming's *The Mirrour of Di-*

vine Love UnVail'd (1691), placed an "Advertisement" at the end of the volume to explain to the reader the problems with the text.

> The Author of the preceding Papers having been absent all the time of their being in the Press, and that at such a distance as to be wholly incapacitated for Revising any of them, the Candid Reader is therefore desired the more favourably to construct of whatever Omissions or other Defects he may Observe therein, and to judge of them as Typographical Errata's, which it's hoped the judicious will easily excuse.[14]

Fleming (1661–1716), who was born and educated in Scotland, had kept a small pocketbook manuscript volume of his verse, containing pieces written between 1670 and 1685, carefully titled and dated. During those years, in 1679, Fleming went to Holland, where he studied at Leyden and Utrecht; in 1682 he completed his long poem "Naturs Sermon" in Rotterdam, where his father was the minister for the Scottish church; Robert the younger was ordained in 1688, and he then returned briefly to England, where he was a private chaplain in an unknown family before returning to Leyden in 1691/92.[15] One can speculate that it was during his stay in England that he had contact with Salusbury, a publisher of theological treatises and also the weekly paper the *Flying Post*.[16]

The reason Fleming's publisher may have had difficulty in producing a clean text in the absence of the author may be explained in part by the condition of the little manuscript volume containing the poems that appeared in print. It is completely written over, including the flyleaves and covers, and the volume reverses halfway through. In "An Advertisement" in the manuscript volume, Fleming explains, "The Poems contained in this manuscript, being at severall times & Occasions either composed or collected, which makes them to be set down so very disorderly, that even to my selfe they appear confused & cannot be much more to others, if they chance to see them: I have therefore thought fit to set down the Titles of those composed by my self, to distinguish them from the rest, (which are collected cheifly out of Cowley, Herbert & Quarles)."[17] Other places in the volume also include helpful hints for reading the manuscript text: "all these following verses which are interlined, being of a diverse nature from the rest, are to be read separately," he warns in one place (32v); in another spot Fleming inserts a symbol with a note, "these lines must be read & come in after this mark" (37r).

Margaret Cavendish, who likewise was unable to be in England to oversee the production of her 1650s texts, complained in the "The Epistle" of *The World's Olio* (1655) that while she herself was not very good at spelling, the problems with her publications were caused by the "negligence of those that were to oversee it":

> For by the false printing, they have not only done my Book wrong in that, but in many places the verse Sense is altered; as for surfets, sercutts, wanting, wanton . . . and many other words they have left out besides, and there is above 2 hundred of those faults; so that my Book is lamed by an ill Midwife and a Nurse, the Printer and Overseer.[18]

The poet and essayist William Walsh was saved from a similar textual disaster by having an experienced friend in London offer to oversee the production: in 1693, John Dryden wrote to Walsh, "Send me your Booke, I will take care to correct the press; & to have it printed well" (Dryden, *Letters,* 62).

Let us look at an author's experience closer to our own, the author of a scholarly, critical text, one with illustrations and an index. A good extended example of the demands, cost, and perils of this type of publication versus manuscript circulation can be found in the diaries of Ralph Thoresby, the antiquarian and a member of the Royal Society, who resided in Bulmer, outside Leeds. Thoresby, who had assembled an impressive collection of prints, manuscripts, coins, and medals, finally yielded to the petitions of friends to publish the pieces he had compiled between the late 1670s and 1700s. His script texts had circulated in the 1680s among his learned friends and members of the Royal Society; he had even occasionally printed short pieces in the *Philosophical Transactions*. In the 1690s, he began a specific text on Leeds and its environs, and in 1711 he records in his diary,

> I walked to Berwick-in-Elmete, to consult my old friend, the parson, about my MS, concerning which I have of late received so many letters and solicitous requests from my friends for the publication, that considering the infirmities which I perceive growing upon me, I cannot but look upon as a memento of my own mortality, and its miscarriage, if not timely prevented.[19]

The manuscript text as memento mori, the printed word as everlasting life—even in his choice of metaphors, Thoresby appears to be the ideal example of the turn to modern technology as a practical and emotional advancement in the culture of authorship.

Thoresby, as a member of the Royal Society, had some experience in subscription publications and printing short pieces. For this massive project involving decades of research, he managed to secure not one but three London printers and engravers in the task of producing this illustrated text. Finally, in 1712, he set off for London: "Having taken leave of my dear wife and children, and besought the divine protection and blessing upon them and me, I began my journey in the company of my cousin Alderman Cookson. . . . We enjoyed ourselves very agreeably in discourse of certain books and their authors" (2:94). On his arrival in London, he took lodgings with his bookseller, Mr. Atkins, who had handled and received most of the subscription fees underwriting the production of the project and who resided over his shop in St. Paul's churchyard. That Sunday morning, after attending church, Thoresby "was at all the three presses, correcting or hastening them, and directing the engravers, which took up the former part of the day" (2:130). His labors continued in this daily fashion: "Morning, rose by five; wrote in Diary; was at church, but afterwards writing for the press till almost blind; scarce moved from my seat till near three, then walked to both the printers" (2:131).

Despite his personal diligence, however, the material realization of authorship no longer depended on his labors alone. On 3 February 1713, the diary entry states: "Read; surprised with the account of Mr. Bowyer's house being burnt, and 5000 £. damage in books; and amongst the rest, about twenty sheets of mine, that were printed at that press, which will retard the publication" (2:182). The next days were spent "in close at work to repair the damage done by the fire at London, revise some sheets."

The work of the volume continued through 1713, after Thoresby returned to Yorkshire. Getting the materials to the printers now involved a network of friends for their conveyance back to London: "Morning, read; then finishing another sheet, and sending it to Mr. Gale, who, after perusal, franks it to the press" (2:186) or "Sent two sheets to the press by Mr. Fenton" (2:197). Print production did involve the family, too: "I had son Ralph's help in collating the print with the manuscript pedigree" (2:203).

In 1714, Thoresby again traveled to London to supervise production, only to be greeted with more ominous news. "Was concerned at the bad news concerning the undertaker [of the project], Atkins, and my own book; [he] is said to be absconded." Hastening to St. Paul's churchyard, Thoresby discovered Atkins' "house disposed of, and his shop to be let. . . . [I] called in vain, at the printers." On the following day, he tracked down Mr. Nutt, the printer, and "heard yet more melancholy tidings from him and Mr. Ross, about Atkins' mismanagement" (2:208). After a few weeks, the entry reads: "Morning with Mr. Dale to meet with the creditors of Mr. Atkins relating to this book" (2:214). Finally, the absconding Atkins returns: "Morning . . . walked to Mr. Atkins' lodging; lost most of the forenoon with him, being at a sad dilemma to get the matter concluded betwixt him and Mr. Nutt, the printer, it being almost impossible to keep the one sober (at least capable of business) till the other gets out of his bed" (2:224–25).

Thoresby got in the habit of rising quite early, in order to catch Mr. Atkins in bed, "else [there was] no meeting him." Subsequent days were spent arguing over copy money (2:226) and how much it would cost to add engravings of pedigrees. The main part of the problem was that Thoresby's book was being published by subscription but Atkins, who received most of the money, failed to advance a promised fifty pounds to Thoresby and furthermore had assigned Thoresby's "property in books" (author's copies) as payment to the printer Nutt (2:235). Almost every day contains a reference to "at the printers" or "work interrupted by Atkins, who was drunk in passion as well as liquor," or "walked to St. James Park, but missed Mr. Boulter, called at Mr. Pingos the engravers and at Mr. Nutts, the printers; found all at a stand, through the indisposition of Mr. Addison, the compositor," interspersed with remarks about his own work on the "tedious index" (2:248, 255). Thoresby wearily summarized his adventures in London publishing as an expensive disappointment: "Instead of £40 profit, the two journeys cost me above £50" (2:228). This section of his journal ends before the publication of *Ducatus Leodiensis* in 1715; perhaps exhausted by his efforts, Thoresby does not resume his diary until 1719.

Ducatus Leodiensis was the scholarly work of decades, which enjoyed learned readership in script and took nearly four years of persistent, determined personal involvement on the part of its author to see its way into print. How many authors, whose texts already enjoyed a positive, responsive audience in script form, would have had Thoresby's time, finances, and sheer determination to make the change to the new technology?

Admittedly, Thoresby's may seem to be a particularly rocky path to print. However, accounts of publishing disasters, once one begins looking, are not that unusual. We also forget the effect of natural disasters during this particular period on the world of literature and publishing. We find

John Collings, in his dedication of *Par Nobiles* to the countess dowager of Exeter, noting, "The Copy of these sheets were in the Stationers hand more than two years since, and unhappily (through his Slowness) perished in your *dreadful Burning,*" by which he meant the Great Fire of London, a forgotten event in the history of the book, which surely devastated a generation of aspiring authors. The stationers had stored their books in the crypt of St. Faith's: "the burning roof of St. Pauls broke through and the contents were destroyed," according to John Evelyn, "burning for a week following, with an estimated loss to the stationers of £200,000" (Lynch, *Jacob Tonson,* 7). Plomer declares that "the chief printing houses and booksellers' shops, with all their contents, were destroyed, and the ashes of books and manuscripts were carried by the wind as far as Eton and Windsor."[20]

The numerous examples of dishonest booksellers, incompetent printers, and those natural disasters to which all advanced technologies seem heir highlight the minimal inducements to embrace print authorship in the 1690s and early 1700s, with its requisite travel, expenses, difficult technicians, lack of financial reward, and the sheer tedium of correcting. All these practical difficulties were compounded tenfold when the author did not accompany his or her manuscript to London. The publishing experiences of the American theologian and natural philosopher Cotton Mather, whose writings were published both in London and in New England during the 1690s and early 1700s, demonstrate some of the acts of textual violence done to manuscripts as they were transformed into print. Mather's literary career illustrates not only the difficulties of securing and using print technology for the author of this period but also some of the problems for the readers of texts sometimes radically altered by print.

Mather firmly believed that it was his Christian duty to write and to publish his writings widely, even recording in his diary a vision of an angel instructing him to write books "not only in America, but also in Europe, publishing."[21] In the excellent article "Cotton Mather Published Abroad," D. N. Deluna explores the spiritual and psychological investment Mather had in seeing his manuscripts in print in London. For Mather, London publication was a mark of God's plan for him; Deluna's analysis of Mather's spiritual crises also provides an excellent source for the material obstacles Mather faced in his attempt to fulfill his publishing destiny and the misfortunes that befell his texts on their pilgrimages to London.

As Deluna notes, even though more than one hundred pieces of Mather's had been printed in Boston by 1700, Mather "felt that God's special providence should conduct business for him" in securing a London printer (145). Mather left the oversight of the material details to friends and relatives visiting London, who apparently handled the matter somewhat haphazardly. The resulting misfortunes, both personal and textual, seriously alarmed Mather: "London success would have signalled his dutiful fulfillment of a divine plan; failure, one the other hand, could mean that this plan had been compromised or that the calling had been mistaken altogether" (147). Judging from the events surrounding the London publication of his texts, even for this passionate believer in the power of print, Mather must have felt it required an act of God to be printed in London.

Mather sent numerous manuscripts to London in search of a printer. In his diary, Mather records in 1697 regarding "The Concerned Christian": "I must send it into *London,* for its Publication; and therefore I am waiting upon the Lord, unto whom the *Book* is devoted, for Direction of his Providence, about what remains to be done" (1:253). In 1713, he records that this text "has been destroy'd by the Avarice and Perfidy of the Men in whose hands the Copy was fallen" (2:208), and that manuscript apparently never was printed (Deluna, 148). Sometimes manuscripts would vanish into London for years, only to surface later and be printed. Mather had a friend visiting London track down one such manuscript text: through the friend's efforts, the manuscript had "a *Resurrection* from the *Dead,*" Mather records, and appropriately enough it was published in 1701 under the title *Death Made Easy and Happy* (1:403).

Surely the strangest route from author to publisher, from manuscript to print, however, must have been the one followed by Mather's text *Batteries Upon the Kingdom of the Devil,* which was printed in 1695. Deluna offers an extended reconstruction of events: in the mid-1690s the ship carrying the manuscript was seized by French pirates—real rather than literary. "Fortunately a connoisseur of pious literature was on board the taken ship," Deluna observes, and he persuaded the pirate captain to give him the manuscript. At this point, the manuscript was sent to an acquaintance in London, who showed it to another friend who was a specialist in the subject, who turned out to be none other than Nathanael Mather, the author's uncle; recognizing the handwriting and style, Nathanael Mather wrote a preface narrating the text's strange journey and found a printer for it (149–50). While Mather regarded its long and bizarre career as a mark of God's special dispensation and Providence in looking after the welfare of the text, we can also see in this example an extreme case of the vicissitudes of getting into print.

As late as 1712, Mather was still seeking a London publisher for "Biblia Americana," which he had mentioned as forthcoming in 1702 in *Magnalia Christi Americana*. This manuscript surfaces in the opening letter of the series of thirteen letters Mather sent to Dr. John Woodward and Richard Waller, secretary of the Royal Society in London in 1712, mentioned earlier.[22] These letters detailed Mather's observations of curious natural phenomena in America, compiled over two decades; in the first letter to Woodward, he devotes the opening section to lamenting the lack of interest of London presses in "Biblia Americana" and wishing that "your presses would return to print something else besides your *Politicks,* and serve to better purposes than to vent the *Ill Humours* of Your Nation" (quoted in Levin, 759).

"Biblia Americana" eventually did find a London publisher, but, interestingly, the letters making up "Curiosa Americana" and twenty-six other letters sent to the Royal Society were never published. The *Journal Book* of the Royal Society for 16 July 1713 states that

> Mr Waller produced a Letter he had received from Mr. Cotton Mather, dated Boston in New England, Dec. 1 1712, giving Notice of a MS he had sent containing several Letters concerning several Natural Curiosities and Observations observed by him in New England, with a desire of being Chosen a Member of the Royal Society. After which several Places in the MS were turned to and read, concerning some Plants, Observations on the Rattle-Snake, and of Rain-bows. . . . It was ordered that a Correspondence with him should be cultivated, he being judged a very inquisitive and proper Person for that Purpose; and Mr. Waller was ordered to draw up a Letter in answer to his against the next meeting. (Sterne, "Colonial Fellows," 200)

Waller wrote to Mather on 22 July 1713 announcing, "I shall think my selfe happy in cultivating a Philosophical Correspondence with so candid and learned a Person," and he promised to nominate him for the society.[23] Waller also circulated the manuscript of "Curiosa" among interested fellows. We find that James Petiver, who succeeded Waller on his death in 1715, wrote to Mather that Waller had lent him the manuscript after it had been read to the fellows; Petiver found the contents of sufficient interest to make copies of it for his own use.[24] Perhaps Waller's unexpected death in 1715 prevented the publication of the papers in *Philosophical Transactions*; in any event, the letters circulated widely in several manuscript copies but were never printed.

Mather also did not fare well in terms of the production of the texts that were taken by London publishers. As mentioned before, *Magnalia* was riddled with errors, but at least it conveyed, even if imperfectly, its original thesis. John Dunton's production of *Wonders of the Invisible World,* on the other hand, demonstrates the power of the printer to transform the text of the author. Dunton secured the account of the Salem witch trials after its Boston printing in October 1692, postdated 1693; his London edition brought out in December 1693 is described by one of Mather's commentators as showing "the classic evidences of hasty production, including scrambled pagination and typeface variations."[25] As Cook points out—perhaps overstating the case a bit—Dunton also redesigned the title page of the Boston edition in order to highlight the sensational aspects of the subject matter, emphasizing by the use of large black type "TRYALS," "Several Witches," and "NEW-ENGLAND," in contrast to the more discreet italics of the main title, *The Wonders of the Invisible World.*

In his second edition, however, Dunton not only recast the title page but also heavily edited the contents. Dunton removed "all theological discussion explaining Mather's position" and emphasizing instead the accounts of the persecution of the accused; the resulting "abridgement," in Albert Cook's opinion, makes the author appear to hold a position completely in opposition to what he had originally written. "Through no fault of his own," Cook concludes, "Mather ceases to be a serious theologian struggling to make sense out of circumstances fast getting out of hand; he becomes, instead, a rabid witch-burner" (306). To add a final insult to Mather's original text, Dunton announced a "new edition" on 15 June, *A Further Account of the Tryals of the New-England Witches, from Mr. Increase and Mr. Cotton Mather's New Discourse*—as Cook points out, despite the advertisement and the title page, the contents contain nothing by Cotton Mather but instead consist of a reprint of a pamphlet by Deodat Lawson combined with Increase Mather's *Cases of Conscience.*

One could deduce that problems with securing a publisher and overseeing the final product would naturally be the result of the author being at such a distance from the printer. We find complaints similar to those expressed by Thoresby and Mather, however, by writers living much closer to London. In Dunton's unpublished correspondence, one finds several letters from frustrated or apprehensive authors. In 1709, J. Ellesby wrote to Dunton, "I Begg of you not to alter any ye Title page; for I do not love a stuft and turgid stile, whc Printers are commonly fond of, thinking every word they insert of their own, will bring them in, a penny extraordinary."[26] Ellesby continues that he fears such proposed changes to the title would alter the intent of his piece, making it "look too much like a Personall Reflection & Reproach, which I have industriously avoided thinking it sufficient to expose Vice, without bearding hard on ye memory of those, yt have benn guilty thereof." Furthermore, Ellesby declares,

> I desire my Papers may be Printed by themselves; for I do not love Tacking; & leave them to take their own fate in the world . . . & therefore if you intended to make any other use of them, besides ye bare Printing of them, you will disappoint my Intention & I must Disown it, for our Zeall agst Vice ought not to transport us to what is undecent & besides ye meritts of ye cause. (Sig. 147r)

Such freedoms with authors' texts—as seen in Dunton's treatment of Mather's Salem witch trial texts and those that Ellesby feared for his text—could be taken by Dunton because the printed text was the property of the printer or bookseller.[27] In such instances, there was little an author could do other than protest he or she had been misrepresented and, as Ellesby threatened to do, to disown the work.

Nor can the blame be laid at Dunton's door alone. When one examines the correspondence of late-seventeenth-century authors, one finds a litany of minor complaints about the process of getting into print and this problem of being misrepresented by the booksellers' alterations. John Evelyn wrote to Richard Waller in 1698 to apologize for the text of his that Waller was correcting and editing for reprint in *Philosophical Transactions,* lamenting that "printers' errors" compounded with those of the author to produce a very faulty text.[28] In a similar vein, we find Mary Chudleigh, who resided for most of her life outside Exeter, using her letter "To the Reader" that prefaces her *Essays Upon Several Subjects* (1710) to explain her problems with the control of her text once it had been printed. In 1699, Chudleigh had composed and circulated *The Ladies Defense,* a spirited satire written to confute and confound John Sprint's stridently patriarchal wedding sermon *The Bride-Womans Counsellor* (1699); *The Ladies Defense* was first printed in 1701 in London by John Deere (or Deeve). According to Chudleigh, when

Bernard Lintot decided to reprint his edition of Chudleigh's *Poems on Several Occasions* (1703), he envisioned a different volume than the author did.

> [Mr. Lintot] desir'd me to permit him to add to'em a Dialogue I had in the Year 1700, written on a Sermon. . . . I refusing for several Reasons, to grant his Request, he, without my Knowledge, bought the Copy of the Bookseller who formerly Printed it, and, without my Consent, or once acquainting me with his Resolution, added it to the Second Edition of my *Poems.*[29]

Chudleigh continues that not only did Lintot disregard her wishes, but he also compounded the errors made in the first printing. In the first printing, the preface was "so mangl'd, alter'd, and considerably shortned that I hardly knew it to be my own: but it being then publish'd without a Name, I was the less concern'd." When Lintot reprinted it as part of her *Poems,* he omitted "both the *Epistle Dedicatory* and the *Preface*; by which means, he . . . left the Reader wholly in the Dark and exposed me to Censure" (248). There was no other recourse, however, other than such protests (also printed by Lintot), which are a not-at-all-uncommon feature at the start of revised editions and collected works printed between 1690 and 1710.

In our earlier examples of authors who were outraged by pirated or unauthorized publication of their manuscripts, the common complaint was that the text was corrupt, inaccurate, and not representative of the author's work. In the example of Cotton Mather, who passionately desired and devoutly believed in the blessings of print technology, one can see graphic evidence of the loss of control by the author over the format, content, and even the attribution of manuscript materials. Even when one lived in the same country as the publisher, as the example of Chudleigh suggests, the author could effectively lose control over the materials.

Looking at the experiences of print authors such as Thoresby and Chudleigh, can one really say that this is a more "democratic" technology at this point in its development for the writer? Despite an increase in the number of presses, it was still a technology that required either residence in London or the freedom to travel and the finances to support it. Print cannot, under these conditions, be viewed as a more "democratic" opportunity for those living in Leicestershire or Gloucestershire, or in Scotland or Ireland before 1695, where only a single press could be legally in operation. There is also a real question whether the shift from social authorship to commercial was more democratic or easier for women living virtually anywhere, with little financial or social independence to deal with a bookseller directly. By denying the significance of script authorship, manuscript circles, and social texts, we have in the name of democracy apparently disenfranchised the participation of the majority of the literate population of the period. While celebrating the advance of technology, we have tended to ignore the material conditions of early modern authorship and the dynamics of various types of literary technology; by not appreciating that the existence of an improved technology does not necessary indicate the use of it, we have inflated its importance for different classes or types of authors. And finally, by focusing on the benefits of the new, we have overlooked the very real new obstacles it created for social authors who, unlike the hack writers who lived with the booksellers and were provided with their materials, sought publication for reasons other than financial ones, often at their own expense.

Nor do we yet have a clear sense of the different types of experiences of authorship, from Aphra Behn and Dryden, who negotiated directly with printers and booksellers for the best price, to William Walsh and Mary Chudleigh, who were able to involve a professional writer in assisting in the production of their texts, to Arise Evans and Cotton Mather, who trusted that God would oversee the production. Although we are starting to develop an understanding of the dynamics of being a hack writer—of living with a bookseller or printer, being provided with books, paper, and work space, and producing text on assignment—we are still in the dark concerning the practices of authors who sought a publisher but not an income from writing. We are still in the process of constructing a history of the social text, as it existed in its original context and social moment and then as it moved into print culture.

FIVE

Getting into Print

Literary Life outside
London

In 1662 an Act of Parliament was passed restricting its exercise [the art of print-ing] to London, the two Universities, and York. The Act continued in force till 1679, was renewed in 1685, and finally expired in 1695, notwithstanding the ef-forts of the interested monopolists to keep the press in fetters.

W. H. ALLNUTT, "English Provincial Presses, Part III"

In 1695, there was no tradition of provincial printing. The existing provincial booksellers were unable, for lack of skill and equipment, to set up as printers even had they wished to do so; had they succeeded, they could hope for no more than small and uneconomical local markets for their books.

JOHN FEATHER, *The Provincial Book Trade in Eighteenth-Century England*

In the preceding essays, we have been looking at authors who either were willing and able to go to London with their manuscripts, had friends or relatives there to oversee production, or, like Cotton Math-er, had a strong belief in God's interest in the publication of their texts. What of the authorial population living outside London who could not travel and had no London connections? What we find, as we have already seen, is a still active culture of manuscript circulation and limited publication by presses outside London for that group of authors we classify as "literary."

Our literary histories have tended to suggest that the only reasons for not embracing print were psychological and social inhibitions. Factors such as the writer's gender or class or combination of the two are prominently discussed as barriers to full participation in the new technology, in the new experience of authorship.[1] Such psychologically based historical analysis of authorship, which typically focuses our attention on the individual author, often overlooks the material world in which that writer worked and often overlooks or devalues the advantages of the older model of being an author—script texts and a controlled readership—in particular for women writers but also for any writer living outside London. As we have seen in the previous essay, even having access to London and the finances to support travel and the production of a print text did not make it an easy project for the social author.

As the nineteenth-century enthusiast W. H. Allnutt noted,

> From the time of Henry VIII, Royal Proclamations, Decrees of Star Chamber, the powers given the London Company of Stationers, and (under the Long Parliament) the appointment of Licensers of the Press, placed such great restrictions upon the exercise of the art of printing, that it is only by counting certain privileged and private presses, we are enabled to enumerate twenty centres of Provincial printing down to the practical emancipation of the art in 1695.[2]

As John Feather's study of the provincial book trade in the eighteenth century puts it more succinctly, before the lapse of the Licensing Act in 1695, its "overall effect [was] of confining commercial printing, and hence publishing, to London" (1).

No less important for us to remember, London also controlled the sale of books in the countryside, thus having an effect not only on provincial authors but also on provincial readers of printed texts. As Feather observes,

> The organizational structure which had evolved under licensing, and its retention and indeed reinforcement after 1695, put the provincial booksellers into an essentially dependent relationship with the London trade. The Londoners were the sole source of supply of all the books they published, and often went to considerable trouble to ensure that the country booksellers did not become sharers in such books. (4)

As we have seen in the essays concerning the continuation of manuscript practices during the latter part of the seventeenth century and well into the eighteenth, one way provincial authors and readers dealt with the realities of print production and the marketing of books was to create and reproduce literary texts themselves, socially rather than commercially. Indeed, without the presence of a manuscript literary culture such as we saw with the Astons in Lincolnshire or John Chatwin in Leicestershire, a provincial area that relied solely on print for its intellectual and literary circulation would be stagnant: when speaking of the intellectual and literary culture of a provincial community, it is essential to remember how much of it was based on the exchange of manuscripts, how much the reader's experience of literary culture was transmitted through manuscript copy, not print. Thus, although it is significant that Feather found that there were few "towns of any size in which books were not available," those critics concerned with the impact of print on authorship do not appear to have asked what type of books these were, and their declarations seem to be going too far when it is asserted that in the latter part of the seventeenth century "writing and literacy become strongly identified with print, and the Restoration had a sense of a world overflowing with the productions of the press" (Peters, *Congreve,* 15, 17). Given the pragmatics of obtaining printed books and of having one's texts printed, such assertions that literate culture was identified with and generated by print fly in the face of the practical realities of a literary person living outside London.

If an author living outside London with no contacts there did desire to see his or her works in print, what were the options? There were, of course, presses outside London during the late seventeenth century. The presses at the two university cities, Oxford and Cambridge, come first to mind, but there were also presses in Edinburgh, Glasgow (from 1638), York (from 1509), Dorchester (William Churchill, 1659–88), Exeter (Abisha Brocas, 1655–74), Salisbury (John Courtney, 1650–64), and Colchester (William Hall, 1663); there were also presses at Finsbury, Exeter, Newcastle, Durham, and Bristol that were active during the Civil War but disappeared afterwards.[3] As is discussed a little later, there were also presses in Wales, devoted to the publication of Welsh texts.

What types of materials did these provincial presses publish? Would a budding poet or essayist find a printer for his or her volume outside London? Given the highly restricted market for texts controlled by London booksellers, what did provincial printers and booksellers buy and sell? It becomes quickly apparent on a survey of Plomer's *Dictionaries* that, although there are numerous booksellers in university and cathedral towns, there are very few printers and that the entries for the provincial booksellers producing books are typically quite short, often encompassing the production of only one or two titles over one or two years.

If one takes a survey of printers and booksellers residing outside London or the university cities, some interesting patterns of professional behavior appear, which suggest the extent to which the press was utilized by various classes of authors living in the provinces. In Bristol, Jo. Alexander was credited only with a broadside, *Sad and lamentable cry of oppression . . . in . . . Bristol* (1682). A bookseller named Caldecot in Stamford, Lincolnshire, was "only known from the imprint to a sermon by G. Topham, entitled *Pharisaism disply'd*, 1690" (Plomer, *1668 to 1725*, 63); J. Chamberlain in Bury St. Edmunds published *New English Examples to be turned into Latine* in 1685 for use in Bury School (66); and Robert Chown in Northampton was likewise known only for having had printed *The Speech of Robert Clerk, Esqu. Deputy Recorder of Northampton to the Mayor elect For . . . 1684* (69). Likewise, we find Robert Hilton of Asbourne credited with only *The Gospel-Call in Metre* in 1688, while in Chester, Joseph Hodgson's single publication was T. Leche's *Danger of Bad Principles* (1712).

Undoubtedly, Plomer's dictionaries leave out titles that these representative provincial printers and publishers may have in fact created. What even a brief survey does suggest, however, is that provincial printers were in general not at all interested in printing what we term literary materials. Although the provincial booksellers no doubt sold such texts, their primary interest was in securing sermons and works of theological and local political interest. The types of authors, therefore, most likely to benefit from the supposed explosion of provincial printing in the first two decades after the licensing act expired were not the literary ones but the theological and polemical ones, as well as the creators of proclamations and public announcements.

It becomes apparent while skimming through Plomer that between 1668 and 1710 even more prolific provincial booksellers handled very restricted types and amounts of texts. Given that many produced only one or two titles, the need for an alternative income for provincial booksellers is quite clear. While we can point to a goodly number of booksellers listed as operating in small towns, amusingly, some appear in Plomer not for the books they sold but for their advertisements for other necessities: William Bailey, a bookseller at Burton on Trent and Wolverhampton in 1685, left behind no trace of the books he handled, but he makes it into Plomer's dictionary because his name appears on a list of booksellers selling patent medicine, which was also the case for one Ashworth in Durham in 1696 and John Ball in Banbury in 1685 (Plomer, *1668 to 1725*, 8, 14, 17). Thomas Butter, a bookseller in Exeter from 1714 to 1720, continued this apparently profitable practice of selling books and medicines, as evidenced by his advertisement declaring,

> (Besides Books and Stationary Wares of all sorts) is sold the best of Mathematical and Sea Instruments, several sorts of Physical Medicine, as Dr. Daff's Elixir Salutis, Stoughton's Elixir Stomachicum, Spirit of Scurvy-Grass Golden and Plain &c. Also the famous Cephalick or Liquid-snuff, prepar'd for the Queen. With Japan Ink, Indian-Ink, Cake-Ink, Ink-powder, Common Ink; Ink-Glasses, Pounce, shining sand; great variety of paper-hangings for rooms; the best of Stampt-Parchment and Paper, Bond &c. at reasonable rates, by Wholesale or Retail. (Quoted in Plomer, *1668 to 1725*, 61)

D. G. Vaisey, in his account of the brief and lamentable career of an unsuccessful Oxford bookseller in the 1680s, notes that "it was normal practice for booksellers in provincial towns to have a stake in some other commercial activity, and even in Oxford the presence of a University did not mean that the business of making and selling books was one which could survive unaided by finance from other sources."[4] The most typical commercial connection in Oxford seems to have been not patent medicines but "that of food and drink," Vaisey finding that several of the university printers prior to 1680 "had held wine licenses from the University" and that Thomas Pembroke, in addition to selling books in 1673, was also an innkeeper. Thomas Young of Shaftesbury, perhaps, like the subject of Vaisey's study, Anthony Stephens, lacked a back-up merchandise: he appears in Plomer's only as "sued by James Courtney, bookseller of London, for the balance of his account" (323).

In these examples, we also see that in addition to the limited number of printers and booksellers available to procure publication for an author's text, the booksellers tended to be printing not what we would consider literary texts but instead theological ones, local political pieces, and medical texts. Even when one looks at the oldest and well-established centers of provincial printing, with the largest output of texts between 1660 and 1710, both the output and the type of materials printed were still limited. Even at York, which along with the two university cities was the only licensed press outside London and which housed Charles I's printing press in 1642 after Charles left London, we can get some sense of the limited opportunity for a literary author to see his or her texts printed locally. The productions of

Alice Broad, Stephen Bulkley, and his son John Bulkley, which span from 1660 to 1690, are worth looking at in some detail, especially in comparison with that of John White, who married Alice Broad's daughter Hannah and dominated the York printing scene from 1680 to 1715.

Alice Broad was the widow and successor of Thomas Broad, who had been set up as the official printer by the city corporation under the Puritan general Lord Fairfax between 1644 and 1650; Broad replaced the king's printer, Stephen Bulkley.[5] Shortly after Alice Broad inherited her husband's business in 1660, an act passed in 1662 "for regulating of printing and printing-presses" contained a proviso that excluded York, as long as "all books of divinity there printed should be first licensed by the Archbishop of York . . . and all other books whatsoever there printed should be first licensed by the person to whom the licensing thereof did appertain according to the Act" (quoted in Davies, 89). The first book printed by Alice Broad was *Judah's Restitution* (1661), a sermon by Joseph Hunter given before Sir Christopher Tuner, baron of the Exchequer; the only other book printed in 1661 was *The Duke's Desk newly broken up,* by William Lovell, "Gent. and Traveller," which turns out to be "divers rare receipts both of Physick and Surgery, good for men, women, and children. Together with several Medicines to prevent and cure the most pestilent Diseases in any Cattell," continuing the tradition of linking booksellers and patent elixirs (Davies, 90).

In the seven years she printed texts, Alice Broad produced seven works, all of which followed this same pattern. In 1662 and 1663, she published accounts of the visitation of the archbishop of York and two sermons by Thomas Bradley, the prebend of the cathedral and former chaplain to Charles I. Her final text, which appeared in January 1667, was by Robert Wittie, a physician, on the medicinal effects of different types of water: *Scarbrough-Spaw, or a Description of the Nature and Vertues of the Spaw at Scarbrough . . . also a Treatise of the nature and use of Sea, Rain, Dew, Snow, Hail, Pond, Lake, Spring, and River-Waters . . . to which is added a short Discourse Concerning Mineral Waters.* One feels that a poetically inclined author would not have received much of a welcome from Alice Broad.

In 1662, Stephen Bulkley (who began as a printer in London in 1639) resumed his business in York, from which he had been forced by the parliamentary city government, and continued his trade there until his death in 1680.[6] In 1666, he was indicted by the assizes for printing libelous ballads, but the grand jury apparently ignored the indictment (Davies, 98); Plomer says that Bulkley drew the attention of authorities in 1666 for printing *An Apology for English Catholics* (*1641 to 1667*, 39). During the next eighteen years, Bulkley printed only ten texts, seven of which were sermons (four were by Thomas Bradley); he also printed *A Catalogue of all the Mayors and Bayliffs, Lord Mayors and Sheriffs . . . from King Edward the First*, a life of Thomas Morton, bishop of Duresme, and *The Several Ways of Resolving Faith in the Roman and Reformed Churches* (1677). Bulkley was described in 1666 as earning "but a poore livelyhood, a man well beloved amongst the ould cavaleers and an object of charity," a sad commentary on the vitality of print in the only licensed press outside London and the university towns (quoted in Plomer, 39).

His son John, who ironically is described by Davies as "neither so enter-prising nor so successful as his father," produced exactly two pieces between 1684 and 1690. One was, again, an account of the visitation by the arch-bishop of York, this text distinguished by being done in black letter, "wretchedly printed" (Davies, 105). His only other production was a sermon.

John White appears quite prolific in contrast to his predecessors and contemporaries in York. Marrying at middle age into the Broad family, White moved his trade from London to York and took over the family busi-ness. His first years of publication in the early 1680s follow exactly the pat-tern we have seen, of printing sermons and medical treatises and other top-ical pieces (for example, a twenty-two-page treatise by Charles Allen, *The Operator for the Teeth, shewing how to preserve the Teeth and Gums from all the accidents they are subject to*, 1685); he also, however, printed several more substantial projects, including Martin Lister's history of English animals (250 pages with nine plates) and *Johannes Godartius of Insects. Done into English*, which had fourteen plates and was taken from the original 1672 manuscript owned by Ralph Thoresby (Davies, 108).

White shows some distinctly independent choices in his publications as well. In 1688, he published Prince William of Orange's manifesto, "which had been refused by all the printers in London, King James having issued a proclamation threatening with severest punishment all who should circu-late or even dare read it," and was as a result confined in Hull Castle. Upon William becoming monarch, White was rewarded by being named "Their Majesties Printer for the City of York and the five Northern counties" in May 1689 (Plomer, *1668 to 1725*, 309).

White's list also seems a bit more promising in terms of a local poet or essayist who wished to see his or her name in print. In addition to printing sermons and medical pamphlets, in 1685 White printed *The Praise of York-shire Ale, wherein is enumerated several sorts of drinks, with a discription [sic] of the Humors of most sorts of Drunckards [sic]*, by "G. M. Gent". This 113-page volume consisted of two long humorous poems in Yorkshire dialect and was popular enough to warrant a third edition by White in 1697. The author appears to have been George Meriton, an attorney at North Allerton (also the grandson of George Meriton, dean of York from 1617 to 1624); Meriton published nine other texts, all in London, between 1668 and 1699 dealing with practical legal topics, such as *The Touchstone of Wills, Testaments, etc.* (1668) and *Landlord's Law* (1681), along with two religious tracts in the 1690s, *Immorality, Debauchery, and Profaneness exposed* (1698) and *Antidote against the Venom of Quakerism* (1699) (Davies, 115–16). Apparently, either Meriton felt that a local press would be more interested in Yorkshire dialect humor than a London one, or he did not wish to intertwine his reputation as a legal author with that of local-color humorist. His brother John Meriton, Davies informs us, "adds one more to the numerous company poets, although of mean rank," and had printed elsewhere a tragicomedy "which had been privately acted by the author and his friends, entitled The Wandering Lover. . . . He is described as the dullest dramatic writer that ever England produced" (116). White does have the dubious honor of printing one drama during his tenure, *The Fall of Tarquin, A Tragedy* (1713), by "W. H. Gent," who was William Hunt, the collector of excise at York; this play, "said to be a most wretched performance, was never acted or printed anywhere but at York" (130).

White also printed two texts "for the Author." The first, in 1696, is described by Davies as "disgusting ribaldry," *Pecuniae Obediunt Omnia. Money does master all Things*; it was reprinted in 1698 in London with the addition of poems by Cleveland and Oldham. Davies suggests that "one of the Meritons is entitled to the discredit of it" (122). The other such text was much less offensive to Davies, *The English Master of Defence: or, the Gentleman's Al-a-mode Accomplishment* (1711), which explained "the true Art of Single-Rapier." In the preface, Zach. Wylde, the author, explains that since he himself was responsible for the cost of printing it, "he had quite altered his measures and design in publishing it to the view of all, but only have such a number printed as would be suitable to his purpose" (128–29).

Thus, in the thirty-five years in which John White successfully plied his trade as a printer in York and later as the king's printer, he produced thirty texts, one of which was a drama, two were volumes of verse, and one was what might be termed belles-lettres—the remainder were sermons by local clergy, accounts of visitations, and medical or natural science texts. These four literary texts were the only ones printed in York in the fifty-five years between 1660, when Alice Broad inherited the press, and 1715, when John White died. There was not a noticeable boom in printing literary texts immediately after the expiration of the licensing act. Clearly, if one had the funds to pay for private printing, one could see even the dreariest drama in print; on the other hand, it does not appear that the Yorkshire poetic community utilized the printing press nearly to the extent that the local clergy and antiquarians did.

Why should this be? Why should it be local ministers and physicians who made the most use of print in the provinces rather than the supposedly isolated poets? One could speculate that the existence of those social literary networks we have seen in the earlier essays—the same type of group, perhaps, that acted John Meriton's play—lessened the attractions of going into print. There was no need to go to the expense of having a printer produce one's texts in order to secure an audience as long as there was a social literary environment, such as that surrounding the young Alexander Pope. For the majority of writers and readers in the period at the turn of the century, literary authorship was still understood as an interactive, dynamic, and ongoing exchange. In contrast, those groups that most utilized the provincial presses display a different dynamic in the type of texts that they printed: a sermon marking a specific event, a declaration of a cure, or a proclamation setting law or policy, all texts designed to end discussion, to claim ownership, or to fix a record of events permanently.

When one looks at presses in the university towns, the picture is a little more promising for the literary author who desired to go into print—but not much. Before we turn to Oxford and Cambridge, it is useful to look at printing in Scotland and its universities. In the case of the University of Glasgow press, which came into existence in 1637 because of the determined efforts of the town council and the university, one finds a rocky shore not only for the literary author but also for the printers themselves, who were battling the monopoly held by George Anderson and his heirs.

The first seventeenth-century printer to work in Glasgow, George Anderson, moved from Edinburgh to Glasgow at the same time the General Assembly met there, and he printed its *Protestation of the Generall Assemblie of the Church of Scotland, and of the Noblemen . . . . Subscribers of the Covenant, lately renewed . . .* (1638).[7] Apart from the Covenanters, Anderson was strongly supported by Zachary Boyd, the vice-chancellor of the university, who between 1638 and 1646 provided the majority of the texts printed by Anderson, including such titles as *A Cleare Forme of Cathechising before the giving of the Lord's Supper* (1639). In his will, Boyd left provision for the publication of his manuscripts: "he was the author of many works, in prose and verse; and the terms of his munificent bequest to the University (which included his library) suggest that he was even more eager to see his unpublished works issued by the University" (Maclehose, 25–26). Strangely enough, despite the money left by Boyd, some "5000 merks to be employed by them for printing [his] works," these manuscripts were never published.

George Anderson did not remain long in Glasgow but returned to Edinburgh. His widow continued his practice, printing in 1648 Boyd's *Psalms of David in Meter*. Meanwhile in Glasgow, Duncan Mun tried and apparently did not succeed in continuing the printing trade, and "from 1649 to 1657 Glasgow had no printing firm" (Maclehose, 39). In 1655, Cromwell had issued an order to "his Highness Concell in Scotland": "[Its members were] impowred to erect and make use of and comand any Presse or Presses there for printing and publishing any Proclamacons, Declaracons, Orders, Bookes or other matter wch they shall think fitt for the publique Service and to prohibit the use thereof by any other persons, or in any Cases where they shall see cause" (quoted in Maclehose, 40). In 1657, Cromwell specifically gave the university the right to print Bibles "in Hebrew Greik Latin English or other language whatsuever with all sorts of buikes relating to the faculties of Theologie Jurisprudence Medicin Philosophie Philologie and all other buikes whatsumever" (41).

George Anderson's son, Andrew, was invited by the city magistrates to assume the role of the printer for the city and university. Again, Andrew Anderson published theological treatises and university documents; again, like his father, he returned to Edinburgh in 1661, becoming the printer for that university and city but leaving Glasgow with none.[8] While acting as the university printer in Edinburgh, he produced in 1671 an edition of the New Testament in black letter that was "so disgracefully inaccurate that the

Privy Council, on the 9th of February, 1671, ordained him 'to receive from the stationers all the copies remaining unsold,' and prohibited him under a penalty of £100 sterling from reissuing it, until it should be revised and a new Title Page prefixed to it" (*Notices and Documents*, 2).

Only three months after this printing debacle, he was granted an extraordinary privilege: he was named the king's printer for Scotland for forty-one years. This meant that he alone was to print

> all and sundry bookes or papers of anie language learned or vulgar . . . and that for the space of fourtie one years, . . . with the sole and onlie power dureing the sd space not onlie of Printing his maiesties . . . acts of Parliat Proclamations Edicts & all other papers and Concernes belong to the sd Kingdome Both also of Printing and reprinting . . . of Bibles in all volumes, with the Psalms annexed thereto, als wiel for the churches of Ingland and Ireland as of Scotland, thrid parts of the Bible, and Newtestaments of whatsoevir volue all bookes of Theologie, Commentaries, Concordances, Books of the Common & Civill law, school authors Grammers Rudiements Psalms Confessions of faith Larger an Shorter Catechisms Kallendars & . . . moreover inhibiteing all Journeymen Printers to take breed instruct or keip in service any Apprentice in the Arte of Printing, without license of the sd Andrew & his forsaids. (Maclehose, 47–48)

The son of one of Anderson's thwarted rivals, James Watson, declared, "By this Gift, the Art of PRINTING in this Kingdom got a dead Stroke; for by it no Printer could print any thing from a Bible to a Ballad without Mr. Anderson's Licence."[9]

This monopoly was fiercely defended by Anderson's widow, Agnes Campbell Anderson, who, according to Watson, "persecuted all the Printers in Scotland; *Robert Sanders* (who succeeded Andrew Anderson in Glasgow about 1668) was fin'd and imprison'd, and had his Doors shut up. And *John Forbes* in Aberdeen (who set up about 1660) was process'd and put to vast Charges."[10] In 1695, Mrs. Anderson came after Watson himself and "prevail'd with the Magistrates of Edinburgh to discharge [his] Working for some Time; and in 1701 obtain'd a Warrant from the Privy Council on a false Representation, to shut up [his] Work-house" (18). Needless to say, given such a climate for printers and booksellers under this monopoly, few literary productions saw the light of day from Scottish presses after the Restoration through the first decade of the eighteenth century, regardless of their authors' wishes.

When one turns to the presses at Oxford and Cambridge, the picture becomes more promising for literary authors, although those presses, too, were
dominated by theological, philosophical, and medical treatises. If one looks
in general at the books produced at Oxford and Cambridge between 1660
and 1710, there are greater numbers of literary texts than we have evidence
for having been produced by provincial city printers, but there is still not
what we would think of as a natural link between the literary author and the
publisher or printer. Consider the implications of the following table:[11]

Dates	Ref. #	Number of works printed
1660–70	#110–143	33
1671–80	#144–163	19
1681–90	#164–191	27
1691–1700	#192–212	20
1701–10	#348–379	31
1711–20	#380–410	30

What were the individual items published in Cambridge between 1660 and
1720? Of the three hundred titles in Bowes' catalogue, four were volumes of
English verse, and two were collections of proverbs. The remainder were
sermons, philosophical and theological treatises, and translations. Of these
volumes of English verse it is important to note, too, that three of them
were collections by Cambridge students and masters commenting on national events: *Hymenaus Cantabridgiensis* (1683), which celebrated the marriage of Princess Ann to Prince George of Denmark and whose contributors
included William Fleetwood, the future bishop of Ely, as well as Matthew
Prior and John Chatwin; *Musae Cantabrigiensis* (1689), on the ascension of
William and Mary; and *Lacrymae Cantabrigiensis* (1695), on the death of
Queen Mary. The final volume of verse produced in Cambridge was *Miscellany Poems* (1691) by Thomas Heyrick, which was "printed for the Author
by John Hayes."

We know from the evidence of manuscript volumes and collections of
manuscript verse to be found in the university libraries that the undergrad-
uates and fellows were actively engaged in literary pursuits. There is little
evidence, however, even in a university town, that printing one's verses was

an easy or automatic goal for a literary author. Indeed, as far as print production was concerned, the most ambitious authors were the clergy.

At Oxford, the situation was not dissimilar. In Madan's *Oxford Books,*
which unfortunately only goes up to 1680, we find that between 1651 and
1680, 1,133 titles were produced (#2150–3283), of which only 5 would be
termed literary materials today.[12] As we have seen with the books produced
at Cambridge, the majority of the literary volumes produced before 1680
were collections of verse on public occasions. To honor Cromwell, in 1654
the press produced *Musarum Oxoniensium* Ἐαιοϕορία, whose effusiveness
was satirized by Thomas Ireland in *Momus Elencticus*; in 1660, the university press produced *Britannia Rediviva,* "the official outburst of joy at the
return of the Monarchy," in which, as Madan notes, twenty-four of the
contributors "changed their minds, let us say, after writing adulatory verse
to Cromwell in 1654," including John Locke and Thomas Lockey, the
Bodleian librarian (112). The final such production before 1680 in Madan's
list was *Univ. Epicedice* (1660), on the death of Henry, the young duke of
Gloucester.

In the case of the individual printers operating after 1680 in Oxford, the
pattern of the domination of print by nonliterary materials is continued.
Anthony Stephens, who operated independently as a bookseller in Oxford
between 1682 and 1684, offered twenty-one titles, most of which were translations: he had four editions of Thomas Creech's translation of Lucretius
produced, one each of Tully, Anacreon, Horace, and Erasmus (Vaisey, 93).
Other than that, he produced a defense of Hobbes, a speech of Sir George
Pudsey, the elements of Euclid, a treatise entitled *Catholick Schismatology,*
and two miscellaneous prose tracts. The only original English literary materials he had printed to sell were Thomas Wood's "Ode on the Death of
Charles II" and *Miscellany Poems and Translations by Oxford Hands,* both in
1685, the last year in which he was in business. Perhaps it says something
about why Oxford booksellers were not eagerly pursuing undergraduate poets for their verse to publish (much less pirating it) when we see that his
creditors seized 236 unsold copies of *Miscellany Poems and Translations by
Oxford Hands* (113).

As suggested before, it is clear that the universities had flourishing manuscript literary cultures, only the tip of which ever appeared in print. For
John Chatwin, discussed earlier, his time in Cambridge clearly was of central importance in his poetic life and provided the one occasion for one of

his poems to be printed, a circumstance that his life in Leicestershire apparently did not. In the case of John Morrice, an example that pushes the outside chronological limits of this study, one can see the allure of the press attracting an undergraduate author and his familiarity with the formulas of print authorship, but in the same text, we find traces of the continuing obstacles for a text to make the transition from a manuscript collection into a printed one. Morrice (1687–1740) left behind an interesting manuscript volume now housed in the Bodleian Library.[13] In the *Summary Catalogue*, this manuscript volume is described as "prepared for the press," but there is no evidence that it was ever published.

Morrice was the son of Richard Morrice, a clergyman at Llanver, Salop, and the grandson of Morgan Morrice, a noted Royalist. Leaving the Welsh Marches for Oxford, John Morrice matriculated in May 1705 at age eighteen and was a scholar at Lincoln College from 1705 to 1714. He took his M.A. degree from Magdalen College, Cambridge, in 1714 and his D.D. in 1728 and held a number of positions before becoming the minister of the Chapel in the New Way, Westminster (1722–36), and a chaplain to the Prince of Wales in 1724.[14]

The volume begins with a carefully laid out title page: "Miscellanae: Or, A Collection of Letters, Poems, and Translations, upon several subjects; by John Morrice, A.B: Scholar of Lincoln-College, Oxon." It contains an "Epistle Dedicatory" to Lady Mary Allstone, a "Preface to the Reader," and nearly one hundred pages of dated letters and poems on the recto sheets of the volume, dated between 1705 and December 1707; on the verso side are poems dating from the mid-1720s and 1730s, along with business notes and drafts of correspondence. Clearly, the volume once intended to be the twenty-year-old's copy text for his printer became the memo book for the forty-nine-year-old poet's record of his subsequent love life.

It is interesting to see how the young Morrice by 1707 had absorbed the conventions of moving gracefully from social to print authorship. In his epistle to Lady Mary Allstone, he declares, "nothing less than a positive command from your Ladyship . . . could have oblig'd me to communicate these following conceptions to the censure of the world. Tho' I'm too sensible, how unworthy my abortive productions are to appear in publick, and to be fil'd upon the Register of time, to expect they should merit me either reward or applause."[15] He continues that the only satisfaction he expects is gratifying her wish, "tho' at ye loss of my reputation, tho' at the expense of my fortune," which suggests, perhaps, that he contemplated having the volume printed at his own expense. In the "Preface to the Reader," Morrice firmly announces, "'Twas no restless desire of appearing in print, no vain, and empty ambition of procureing the denomination of an Author; but rather necessity, than choice, that obliged me to publish these following papers" (9r), a declaration that seems sadly ironic, as does the explanation that follows:

> Some of my particular acquaintance, in whose hands, thro' frequent correspondence, the major part of these trifles were, after such urgent, and almost incessant importunity, and sollicitation to have them made common, concluding their entreaty fruitless, and unprevailing, determin'd and decreed, to commit what they had clandestinely to the press. But, beeing accidentaly inform'd of ye design, I perswaded myself, yt it was the most prudent way, to obviate their endeavours, and put a period to their proceedings, but ordering and digesting ym into yt best method I could, and so letting ym paws, 'till time, and opportunity should offer it self to revise, amend, and correct ye errours. (9r–10r)

At this time, as far as can be found, there is no evidence that any of Morrice's letters or poems were ever printed. Indeed, since the verso sides contain poems and notes written in the 1720s and 1730s, it suggests that Morrice kept the volume in his possession for more than twenty years after it was originally completed for the printer.

What is one to make of this seeming authorial contradiction, of an author who physically prepares a volume for printing and then apparently does not do so? There could be an aesthetic reason: it could be that the young Mr. Morrice thought better of publishing works that he describes as having been "compos'd between the years of twelve, and sixteen" (10r), and which deal with teenage melancholy and peevish love. "Beeing in a melancholy mood, and having neither money in [his] pocket to spend nor books in [his] study to read," he opens one presumably entertaining letter "to a friend, showing how much a countrey life ought to be prefer'd to an University confinement" (46r), which represents the tone of much of the volume. Likewise, having been spurned by "Gloriana," whose previous warmth towards him seems to have vanished while he was absent at Oxford, Morrice declares, "[Her] forbidding lookes, icy, frigid grasps, & sapless kisses; & every thing running so counter to my expectations, yt I was (not-

withstanding all opposition) cast into a deep melancholy" (125r). He includes several mild antifemale pieces to express his disdain for the fickle sex
at this point.

Given Morrice's career in the church, perhaps he felt that his new business was, as he declares in the final letter of the volume, to "adore God, &
not my Mistress." "I'll love his mercy, not her smiles; fear his anger, not her
frowns," he concludes, "[and] admire the ineffable purity and simplicity of
his essence, which is eternal, & will triumph over time it self & not ye fade-
ing charms & declining beauty of her face" (195r). Morrice became curate
of Lamborne, Berkshire, in 1709, then rector of Thorpe-juxta-Newark in
1713; since the majority of the volume deals with his infatuation with the
unresponsive girl he left at home and his subsequent decision to "either kill,
or cure" himself—"I immers'd myself in Epicurism . . . and turn'd all over
Rake" (126r–127r)—perhaps his new calling made him reluctant to publish
his accounts of rejected love.

There also could have been a financial reason for not publishing. Morrice suggests in his dedication that he will obtain "ye loss of my reputation,
tho' at the expense of my fortune" to please Lady Mary, suggesting that he
intended to take the cost of printing, as we saw with William Hunt's play in
York and Thomas Heyrick's 1691 *Miscellany Poems* in Oxford. However, the
contents of the poems and the letters stress that another reason for his melancholy was his lack of funds: in a letter dated 9 September 1706, Lincoln
College, he announces, "Poor wretch'd I! am by some cruel destiny confin'd'
unto a solentary, bookish life; to tumble old dusty Authors or'e and or'e and
stuff my head with names of antiquated Books: surrounded by grining pen-
ury, and hunger, the inseparable companions of want" (46r). At the end of
the volume, in a letter to his uncle in London dated 23 December 1707, he
thanks him for his interest in what the young man's future will be, announcing, "The determination is dubious & tho' it lies in my own brest,
yet 'tis unknown to myself, whether I shall be an Ecclesiastic, or a Layic"
(185r). Such a career choice does not suggest a young man of means, who
would have been able to support the printing of a sizeable volume.

Finally, the latter part of the original volume was composed away from
Oxford, after Morrice had returned to the frigid Gloriana. He signs several
pieces as being from "Gwinerring," and there are short, occasional verses
that mention specific locations in Wales and the Welsh Marches, such as an
epitaph on "old Jedins" of Beguildy in Radnorshire; he also addresses a

letter to "Madam Price" from "Llanvair Hall" in north Wales.[16] Thus, while Morrice might have had the opportunity while still in residence in Oxford to have secured a printer to produce his volume, once he returned to Wales, the opportunities to find a printer diminished considerably.

Ironically, had Morrice been writing in Welsh, his options for publication might have been greater. Geraint H. Jenkins noted that between 1660 and 1709, 215 titles were published in Wales, in Welsh, with 76 of them appearing between 1700 and 1709.[17] The first Bible in Welsh had been produced by subscription in 1677–78; in Jenkins' opinion, the sudden increase in the number of Welsh texts is directly tied to the expiration of the licensing law that permitted the founding of the press in Shrewsbury in 1696 by Thomas Jones. Jones held the royal patent for the publication of Bibles in Welsh, a monopoly he, like the Andersons of Edinburgh, appears to have been eager to extend (239, 232). In common with printers in other parts of country, the presses in Wales in the latter part of the seventeenth and early eighteenth centuries produced mostly religious, didactic materials, including Welsh translations of *Pilgrim's Progress* (1688) and Jeremy Taylor's *Holy Living* (1701); Jenkins observes that "up to a point, it could be argued that the dissemination of didactic and devotional books—the largest single category of literature in this period—reflected ideological considerations and cultural patterns not wholly rooted in Welsh soil. But this does not mean that the books were either alien or unacceptable to the reading public" (52).

In addition to these didactic texts, there was also a market for religious verse; "the addiction of most Welshmen to verse was proverbial. Nothing was more agreeable to his countrymen, wrote Thomas Jones in 1696, than reading and singing Welsh verses" (147). In his *Manual of Welsh Literature*, the Reverend J. C. Morrice surveys the major writers of the seventeenth and eighteenth centuries; the overwhelming majority were devotional poets occupied with transmitting the Scriptures in Welsh.[18] Wales' most famous poet publishing in English, it might be noted, was Henry Vaughan; he published all of his texts in London.

This is not to say that John Morrice was alone in Wales in his propensities to write occasional and amorous verse. We find, for example, a sizeable collection of English verse in manuscript in the Bulkeley papers dating from the 1670s; although the titles suggest religious fervor, the contents suggest a life similar to that described by John Morrice when he turned complete Epicurean. "It would appear that he must have been as drunken a sot and lying a rogue as any in that part of the country," the Victorian commentator on the manuscripts observes.[19] In a poem to his brother, the high sheriff, the poet helpfully declares,

> 2. But I will doe the best I can
>   and uttermost endeavour
> to be a sober civill man
>   and honest of behaviour
>
> 3. I will not drink as I did use
>   nor be intemperate
> men for my company I'll chuse
>   who shalbe moderate
>
> 4. Nor will I walk along the Street
>   with any idle sott
> my company shall be discreet
>   with whom I drink a pott
>
> . . . .
>
> 6. I pray you brother doe not doubt
>   that I will from you shrink
> You know that I can helpe you out
>   If I forbeare to drinke. (33)

This poet also offers 600 stanzas of "Meditations," 220 stanzas on "a Description of Hypocrites," 50 stanzas of "Confessions," ("his candor at times is uncommonly amusing"), and a 43-stanza "Christmas Carol," in addition to anagrams and short pieces on such unpromising topics as "the Swearing & Admittance of the Chancellor of the Excheqr in Ireland. 27 Octo, 1674." Whatever one thinks about the skill of the poet, it is clear that for him and his readers writing verse was a social act and one that engaged considerable energies.

In addition to such surviving collections of English verse, Rev. J. C. Morrice confirms our sense that there was a flourishing manuscript culture in Wales during this period through secondary indicators. One curious example of the extent of manuscript culture in Wales during this period is found in the collection of William Maurice, who died between 1680 and

1690; Maurice is described as "a most industrious collector and transcriber of Welsh manuscripts," and he constructed a library "three stories high, in which he spent most of his time in the study of Welsh literature" (*Wales in the Seventeenth Century*, 344). As Rev. J. C. Morrice observes, given the difficulties for English printers in correctly setting Welsh texts, "many works of [the seventeenth century] and the preceding periods still remain in MS.,—a number out of all proportion to those which have seen the daylight in print" (*Wales in the Seventeenth Century*, 4).

John Morrice's manuscript volume is obviously one of this multitude of literary texts still in manuscript. Even though the expiration of the licensing act in 1696 might appear to open the door for publication for this type of author, and even though it appears that he himself had made the decision to publish, it seems that one or more of a variety of practical considerations—aesthetics, money, geography—intervened. What is interesting, however, as an insight into the world of the social author as it continued into the eighteenth century is that Morrice preserved the volume and turned to it again in the 1720s and 1730s to record, once again, love poetry and occasional verse.

The literary author living outside London or the university towns was obviously affected by the lapse of the licensing act in the increasing flow of printed texts from London that became available in the provinces in the first half of the eighteenth century and in the founding of the first provincial newspapers. However, when one examines the types of texts that provincial booksellers and printers were themselves producing, it does not appear that literary authors found the new technology as immediately appealing or applicable to their practices of authorship as we have supposed. Literary authors, even those in the university towns, continued to rely on that social system of authorship we have discussed before, which had the advantages of being controlled by the author and his or her friends, of being much cheaper than printing, and of providing an ongoing source of literary and intellectual capital, even if not bringing in any commercial benefits. For those writers living outside London, the attractiveness of the new technology of print and the changes in the laws governing its use did not immediately overwhelm the existing system of benefits found in the older forms of social authorship.

SIX

Making a Classic

The Advent of the
Literary Series and the
National Author

Clasick: an author of the first rank: usually taken for ancient authors.
SAMUEL JOHNSON, *Dictionary*

One might well argue that many of the social, manuscript authors encountered in the previous essays are hardly lost "classics" waiting to be
recovered. Whether it was lack of skill or lack of inspiration that kept
these social authors from entering the canon is open to debate; certainly the works of writers such as John Chatwin and Robert Flem-
ming have a legitimate claim on any admirer of seventeenth-century
verse. What is less clearly established by such examples, however, is
the nature of the relationship between being a social, manuscript author and being dismissed as unskilled by subsequent generations. Or,
to reverse the focus of the question, it is unclear what the relationship
is between being in print and being deemed an author of "classic" designation.

In his "Plan and Catalogue of Cooke's Uniform, Cheap, and Elegant Pocket Library" printed in 1794, the publisher John Cooke declared that such an enterprise, the creation of "a complete Library,
comprising all the most esteem'd Works in the English Language, each
printed in the same Type, in the same Size, on the same Paper, and
embellished by the same Artists, was never before attempted in this
kingdom."[1] Like most advertising claims then and now, Cooke man-
ages to stay just within the bounds of truth; *Cooke's Pocket Edition of*

Select British Poets was perhaps the most ambitious literary series of its day, but it was by no means the first. The practice of assembling multiauthor, uniform volume series by booksellers had its beginning in the mid-eighteenth century; the explosion of popularity for the format by the end of that century, along with its subsequent secure place in publishing practices to this day, is a revealing episode not only as an innovative moment in the history of publishing but also as a first step in the creation of a format for national literary histories.

The pervasive use of such marketing methods, which package and present literary materials not as individual works of art but as commodities forming part of a multipiece series to be collected, consumed, and displayed as a unit, also raises questions concerning the ways in which literary aesthetics, a concept of national identity, and the concrete particulars of the economics of writing and reading intersect at certain historical moments. We can use this historical case of the advent of a new method of selling and promoting literary texts in the eighteenth century in order to provide a different perspective on the ways in which current canons of "the classics," or that group of texts the literate portion of the population is presumed to be acquainted with, have been shaped. Investigating the advent of a new method of presenting a work of literature to a commercial public lets us see more clearly the dynamics at play in what appears to be a shift to institutionalize and commodify both the practice of authorship, or the act producing texts, and that of readership, or the act of acquiring and consuming them.

In studying a phenomenon such as a new marketing technique for literary materials, one is also studying the development of a related vocabulary of "commercial aesthetics." Key terms associated with texts found in multivolume, uniform series today, for example, include "classic" and "library." In 1755, Samuel Johnson defined the word *Classick* in the following ways: "1. relating to antique authors; relating to literature . . . 2. Of the first order or rank," with a secondary, separate entry identifying the noun to represent "an author of the first rank: usually taken for ancient authors."[2] Today, we tend to associate the term *classic* with the work itself rather than the writer, but for us as well, the term combines a sense of the historical past and progress towards the present in addition to acting as a critical seal of approval. It was not until Johnson's time, however, that we see the emergence of a new type of British publishing practice—a multivolume, uniform edition series composed of literary works. The stated goal of this new format was to present English literature in a manner to rival that used to preserve the works of classical Greek and Roman writers and in which those "national" literatures were studied in English universities.

The term *classic* when it is applied to an English or American literary text performs a dual signification. It implicitly connects a text simultaneously with the dynamic passage of time and a static standard of critical merit, whether it be in reference to the antique Greek and Roman past surviving up to the present in the Classics Department or a happily imagined projection in an ad in the *New York Times* that a text will be "the classic novel of our times," a work of art that will transcend time and be valued a hundred years from now. This use of the noun also conveys the sense that somewhere along this time line a universal, transcendent aesthetic judgment has surveyed and ranked works hierarchically in terms of merit, using as the base for comparison the standards set by the ancient texts. The term, thus, uses history and the passage of time as an aesthetic hallmark of literary value.

A historical feature to notice about *classic* is that although in the eighteenth century Johnson defined it as though it was to be applied to individual writers and works, for us it is most commonly thought of as applying to a body or group of texts: we have the "classics," which in turn make up the institution the "canon," or that body of knowledge generally believed to compose the materials of significant value in a standard education. Modern publishers clearly market their texts with that notion: we have the Oxford World Classics, Signet Classics, Everyman Classics, Virago Classics, and Penguin Classics, just to name the most obvious.[3] Each of these series comprises several hundred titles, each is primarily designed for classroom use, and each is brought out in either paperback or inexpensive hardback editions. Their domination in the classroom market is so complete that when critics interested in the question of opening up the canon began their assaults upon the academy, it was the study of titles included in these "classic" series that provided the focus of the debate. Indeed, Virago Press was established to provide a counterlist of "classics" written only by women, since the lists of titles produced under that label by the major houses in the 1960s through 1980s produced a definition of *classic* that was almost entirely male.

Thus, for us, the notion of a series is firmly linked with the notion of the "classic" and carries with it the sense that texts included in the series have been certified by an unspecified agency as being of significant aesthetic value or literary merit. However, in the eighteenth century, the origins of the concept of a multivolume series, I will argue, despite the publisher's declarations, have much less to do with an attempt to impose a hegemonic ideology of literary merit than with a response to publishing conditions in combination with an attempt to foster a new type of reading audience for literary texts as entertainment and as a social commodity.

Historical conditions of publishing and printing determined that the marketing of a multivolume, uniform series featuring multiple authors was not feasible in Britain until the mid-eighteenth century. To understand the nature of these first efforts at creating a uniform "package" of national literature, we must turn first to the mundane considerations that faced eighteenth-century booksellers who wished to earn a living at the trade.

The first obstacle facing a British publisher contemplating such a scheme of offering a uniform series of texts by writers both living and dead rather than separate works by a single author was the confused and confusing nature of copyright law in eighteenth-century England. In 1709, the so-called Act of Queen Anne had attempted to control the creation of new monopolies in the book trade by doing away with the concept of copyright held in perpetuity by a purchasing bookseller. This statute appeared to come down in favor of the rights of the author to maintain control of and interest in his or her literary creation; it granted a twenty-one-year copyright to booksellers who held the earlier stationer's copyright on old texts, and a fourteen-year copyright for works by contemporary, living authors, at the end of which time copyright would return to the authors for another term of fourteen years.[4] Despite the 1709 statute, however, London publishers, including the "fathers of English book trade," Jacob Tonson, Bernard Lintot, and Andrew Millar, continued to act as though perpetual copyright did exist as a feature of common law. These major players in the market aggressively protected their purchased stock of texts and dead authors, and cases such as *Millar v. Taylor* in 1767 supported their monopolies on publishing texts to which they had purchased copyright, even after the date for expiration set in the Act of Queen Anne had passed (Patterson, 168–72). Until the latter part of the eighteenth century, any design to publish a large series of complete texts involving a wide range of authors would have been extremely costly, if not simply impossible, given the difficulties arising from the fragmentary pattern of ownership of the copyright scattered among protective booksellers.

Even though, as Marjorie Plant observed, these London booksellers failed in their attempt to return to a formal, recognized law of perpetual copyright in 1724 and 1731, the years in which the limited-term copyright on popular early writers, including Shakespeare and Milton, came to an end, it was not until the Edinburgh publisher Alexander Donaldson's production of James Thomson's *The Seasons* created the landmark case of *Donaldson v. Beckett* in 1774 that the notion of perpetual copyright existing as a feature of common law was ruled out by a narrow vote in the House of Lords (Patterson, 172–79). Interestingly, it becomes clear that both the perceived and imagined roles of the bookseller/publisher, the author, and the audience were involved in reaching the ruling.

On the one hand, the House of Lords was actively opposed to a monopoly of trade in the hands of a few booksellers. "All our Learning will be locked up in the Hands of the Tonsons and Lintons [*sic*] of the age, who will set what price upon it their avarice chuses to demand, till the public becomes as much their slaves, as their own hackney compilers are," observed Lord Camden of the necessity of ruling against the booksellers (Patterson, 178). On the other hand, if booksellers are represented as mercenary commodifiers in this decision, authors are depicted as living above commercial considerations, and the reader is depicted rather like a spectator at a play or event who, after paying the initial price of admission, rewards the writer only with applause. In defending the rights of authors in their literary creations, Camden makes it clear that there were different classes of authors and texts to be considered: "I speak not of the scribblers for bread," ruled Camden, "who tease the press with their wretched productions; fourteen years is too long a privilege for their perishable trash." Copyright is instead designed to protect a different type of writer with a different type of reader. "It was not for gain that Bacon, Newton, Milton, and Locke instructed and delighted the world; it would be unworthy of such men to traffic with a dirty bookseller. When the bookseller offered Milton five pounds for his *Paradise Lost,* he did not reject it and commit it to the flames; he knew that the real price of his work was immortality, and that posterity would pay it."[5]

The effect of this decision, however, was certainly not to revive the practice of amateur coterie writing but, paradoxically, to make it possible for more publishers to produce more editions of writers out of copyright more cheaply and thus to make inexpensive literary texts more profitable. We find another Scot, John Bell, launching what may be termed the first uniform series in the modern sense with his *British Poets,* which saw more than one hundred volumes produced between 1777 and 1789. Better known and respected by literary scholars than Bell's series was the rival London production of Johnson's *Lives of the Poets* (1779–81), followed in due course by the astonishingly prolific Cooke's editions. In the early decades of the nineteenth century, the critic Richard D. Altick recorded the launching of just under one hundred reprint series, identifying 1830 as "the beginning of the era when publishers developed cheap classic libraries as an integral—not merely incidental—part of their lists."[6]

The marketing methods for literary materials that preceded Donaldson's case and Bell's series established the characteristic features of the uniform series and the nature of the appeals made to prospective purchasers. In the mid-eighteenth century, the booksellers made marketing experiments that established certain successful tactics for promoting the sale of literary materials as sources of entertainment and, of course, edification. The practice most obviously related to the phenomenon of uniform series was that of serial publication, of bringing out longer works in parts; one example is *A View of the Universe; or, a New Collection of Voyages and Travels into all Parts of the World,* compiled by John Stevens, which involved seven complete texts published in monthly numbers running from 1708 to 1710 and issued in 1711 in two quarto volumes (Wiles, 87).

Another format was the collection of shorter pieces of occasional verse, lyrics and epigrams in particular, to make up cheap and popular collections. Songbooks, too, some with music, some only with the lyrics, issued by Henry and George Playfair and others make up a good portion of the titles we would classify as "literary" that were published during the Restoration and first decades of the eighteenth century. New issues appeared periodically offering the purchaser "the most fashionable songs sung in court." Finally, in this same pattern, we find numerous "Miscellanies," or collections of mixed prose and verse pieces by various well-known living authors, the most famous of which was Dryden's multivolume *Miscellanies* published by Lintot, in which living writers contributed pieces making up individually titled volumes, which were then gathered together in uniform volumes.

Typically, such texts as these carry their promotional advertising on their title page, where their appeal to the buyer/reader is bluntly set forth. The title pages guarantee the prospective buyer that the contents are, for example, *New Songs and Poems, a-la-mode both at Court, and Theatres, now Extant.*

Never Before Printed (1677), *A New Collection of the Choicest Songs. Now in Esteem in Town or Court* (1676), *The Last and Best Edition of New Songs: Such as are of the Most General Esteem Either in Town or Court. Collected with the Greatest Care, and Printed After the most CORRECT COPIES* (1677), and *The Beau's Miscellany, Being a New and Curious Collection of Amorous Tales, diverting Songs, and entertaining Poems* (1731). In addition to stressing the newness of the pieces (supposedly appearing in print for the first time) and their popularity in fashionable circles, most of these collections included the assurance that "most" of the contents were "written by Persons of Eminent Quality."[7] Thus, in addition to promising entertainment in the form of new, current reading materials to enjoy, the volumes also suggest that their ownership confers a degree of sophistication and fashion with their purchase, offering a taste of aristocratic entertainment style at a reasonable fee as well as being a collectable item.

In this pattern of collecting short pieces from numerous writers and producing them in a uniform set of volumes, we find Robert Dodsley's three-volume collection of verse in 1748, *A Collection of Poems by Several Hands,* to which three more volumes had been added by 1756; the entire six-volume *Collection* then went through numerous editions and outlived its original compiler, Dodsley.[8] Perhaps even more significant as a forerunner of the inexpensive reprint series was Dodsley's *Select Collection of Old English Plays,* which first appeared in 1744 and was revised, expanded, and reedited by Isaac Reed in 1780, then by Octavius Gilchrist and J. P. Collier in 1825–28 to reach thirteen volumes, and finally revised again by W. Carew Hazlitt in 1874.

Dodsley states in his preface to *Old English Plays* that, unlike the ephemeral miscellanies of fashionable occasional verse that stress the new and the current, the contents of his collection are historical documents that demonstrate the range and progress of the English drama. The announced purpose of the collection is to preserve these antique texts from oblivion. He maintains that this is a worthy ambition because such texts demonstrate the history not only of the theater but also of the British nation and national temperament.

"When I first conceived the design of collecting together the best and scarcest of our old Plays," Dodsley announces at the opening of his preface, which was carried over in the subsequent revisions of the project, "I had no intention to do more than search out the several authors, select what was good from each, and give as correct an edition of them as I could."⁹ The design was to "serve as a specimen of the different merits of the writers, and shew the humours and manners of the times in which they lived" (1:xxix). Thus, the collection combines antiquarian interest with a guarantee of quality, the best of the early authors, along with an apparatus to ensure the "perfection" of the volumes and the "entertainment" of the reader. Dodsley included, where possible, a life of the author before each play and, at the beginning of the first volume, a contextualizing brief history of the "rise and progress of the English stage, from its earliest beginnings, to the death of Charles I, when play-houses were suppressed."

There are several noteworthy features in Dodsley's successful multivolume series. The first is the nature of the appeal made to the purchaser—like the contents of miscellanies, these plays are described as difficult to obtain individually, although these texts are obscure because of their age, not their newness. Dodsley dedicated the first edition to Sir Clement Cotterel Dormer, whose collection of first editions of early plays formed the source of the contents; Isaac Reed describes how this collection of early English drama eventually ended up in the hands of David Garrick, who bequeathed it to the nation in the institution of the British Museum.

The second feature of interest is the presentation of the contents as being of importance as historical documents, mirrors of the manners and mentalities of their writers and original audiences. By reading these texts, the buyer is assured, he or she will see what life was like for Elizabethan Englishmen and women. Dodsley states he offers more comedies than tragedies in this collection because "they better serve to shew the humors, fashion, and genius of the times in which they were written" (lxxviii). He describes them as "elegant entertainment" that shows "the progress and improvement of our taste and language."

Isaac Reed, in the preface to his revision of Dodsley, also warns that the plays may cause difficulties for the modern reader of refined taste at the end of the eighteenth century. "The first attempts in any art are always rude and imperfect," Reed warns, "more calculated to exercise the sagacity of an antiquary than to gratify a taste rendered delicate by being accustomed to the improvements which luxury and riches introduce. The polish of modern fashions ill agrees with the barbarity of ancient manners" (xii). However, Reed maintains, a knowledge of these works is essential, "to obtain a perfect knowledge of some of our most esteemed authors." The collection, Reed asserts, also demonstrates that "many beauties had long remained unknown and unnoticed; that fame had not always accompanied worth; and that those who wished for information concerning antient manners would not be able to obtain it so well from any other source" (xv).

Literary merit or pure aesthetic consideration is clearly not the main feature that either Dodsley or Reed believes makes the collection of interest and importance to readers. Rather, the contents are entertaining for their historical dimension and to confirm or, indeed, credential the merit of subsequent generations of writers. In concrete terms, it is also important to note that Dodsley and Reed are able to publish the collection because of the rarity, not the popularity, of the printed texts; these plays were not the property of another bookseller but instead owned in a private collection.

In these introductions, nevertheless, one is also assured that a selection process had been done, that the contents (which change with the different editions) are the "best" work of that particular author. This collection does not use the term *classic* to describe its contents, but the general terms associated with that label are already in place: while one is assured of "entertainment" from the historical character of the pieces, it is also suggested that refined readers can improve their appreciation of modern authors.

When we arrive at the point of John Bell's series, *The Poets of Great Britain*, sometimes referred to as *Bell's British Poets*, which appeared in 109 volumes between 1777 and 1793, we have all the mechanisms for the presentation of bulk literature to a consuming public established.[10] What Bell (and later Cooke) does so splendidly is to refine the key terms associated with the presentation of literary series and to define even more clearly the specific markets for different types of literary products.

As the title page of Stanley Morison's book-length study of Bell suggests, Bell was perfectly situated in the world of literary production to create, promote, and deliver a national literary series. Morison's book is titled *John Bell, 1745–1831: Bookseller, Printer, Publisher, Typefounder, Journalist, etc.* Morison is most interested in Bell as the creator of new typefaces, formats, and printing techniques, and he studies Bell's experiments in the creation of periodical publications including the *Morning Post,* the *World,* the *Oracle, Bell's Weekly Messenger,* and *La Belle Assemblee;* Bell produced three enormous literary series, *Bell's British Theatre, Bell's Poets of Great Britain,* and *Bell's Edition of Shakespeare,* and despite rival London printer Edward Dilly's famous dismissal of *Bell's Poets* to James Boswell as a "little trifling edition" with tiny print, they are all noteworthy in the history of print for their innovative typography and format. In addition to creating these series and the newspaper and periodical publications appealing to a variety of carefully considered reading audiences, Bell also was the proprietor of "Bell's Circulating Library," which Bell's newspaper the *Morning Post* announces "may with great truth be advertised as the most extensive, and most convenient public Library in this kingdom."[11] This library, which Bell after 1780 advertised under the name "Bell's British Library," assured the subscriber for one guinea a year of being lent "Pamphlets, and every Publication that appear[ed], without disappointment or tedious delay," as well as a complete catalogue that would be annually updated and delivered. He also used this location to display his own books before publication (Bonnell, 141). In short, Bell had the wit as well as the facilities to design, produce, advertise, circulate, and deliver literary texts to a readership already established with his periodical publications.

The advertisements for *Bell's British Theatre* and *Bell's British Poets* continue several of the themes found in Dodsley's introduction and expand our knowledge of how reading audiences for different types of literature were defined. As Thomas Bonnell noted in his excellent study of *Bell's Poets of Great Britain,* examining the rivalry this series created between Bell and the consortium of London booksellers that retaliated by commissioning Johnson's series *Works of the English Poets* does much to expand our knowledge of the dynamics of the book trade in the eighteenth century; I would suggest it is also highly revealing of the dynamics of shaping a national literary commodity in addition to setting the precedent for creating a canon of national literature.

In the prospectus describing his project printed in the *Morning Chronicle* on 14 April 1777, Bell announces that "the Plan of this undertaking is to furnish the public with the most beautiful, the correctest, the cheapest, and the only complete uniform edition of the British Poets." As Bonnell states, given the stated design, purpose, and scope of the project, it can be called "the first serious attempt to publish a comprehensive English literary canon." Bonnell has done a tremendous job in analyzing the format and presentation of Bell's series in comparison with that of Johnson's *Works*; what interests me further in reading Bell's advertising and examining his presentation of these texts is the way in which the process of creating a "classic" in the sense of forming a canon is intimately involved with the dynamics of developing a commercial market for literature as a commodity.

What one immediately notices in Bell's promotion of the series is his attempt to appeal to buyers through a number of carefully targeted appeals that are rather different in nature. These editions are both the "most beautiful" and "the most correct": externally, they are desirable objects of aesthetic merit because of their physical presentation, but they are also scholarly in that they provide accurate, edited content. One sees this careful combination of the text as both a collectable commodity and a cultural event throughout Bell's representation of the series in the advertisements. The collectable nature of the series is emphasized in the description of the uniformity of the volumes, the excellence of the production, and the presence of ornamental engravings; the cultural significance of the content is established through implicit comparison with available book series of Latin and Greek texts, that is, the "classics."

These two are neatly brought together in Bell's reference to the "delicate size" of octodecimo for the series, a format "resembling the Elziver editions of the Latin classics." Thus, in format, Bell selected a presentation that had been established for university readers of Latin texts (Bonnell, 139), suggesting a comparison between contemporary British writers and the established classics, while also pointing out the desirability of the small size in terms of books as collectable objects. In an advertisement printed in the *World* on 5 January 1787 under a heading "Travelling Poetick Library," Bell offers "the most classical productions that have been published in this country within a series of four hundred years . . . printed most beautifully with elegant and interesting embellishments." Bell declares that the series, "comprizing together One Hundred and Nine Miniature Volumes . . . [can be purchased] now contained in two small cases, formed like folio volumes, which may be packed with convenience and safety in the inner seat of a post chaise."

One of the principal differences between Bell's publications and that of the London consortium producing *The Works of the Poets* was the nature of the appeal to purchasers with different ambitions. Johnson's *Works of the Poets* was available only in a complete set of 60 volumes costing £7 10s.; with Bell's series one could buy 109 volumes for as little as £8 8s., and, more significantly, one could buy separate issues for a little more than 1s (Bonnell, 139–40). One could buy five different versions of Bell's series: the cheapest was described as "neatly sewed and titled," followed by a bound version in calf with double lettering, then calf with gilt pages that was registered, then calf with gilt pages, with marbled paper. The deluxe luxury version of the series costing £33 was "superbly bound in Morocco" with gilt-edged paper.

One finds this appeal to a variety of classes of readers in all of Bell's series. In an advertisement for *Bell's British Theatre* in the first volume of that series in 1776, Bell lets it be known that "a Few Copies will be printed for the curious, on large Royal Paper," at 1s. each number but that the standard will be 6d.; whichever format one selects, one can be certain that "each of the sizes will bind up uniform with Bell's Edition of Shakespeare, and when finished will form a complete *Dramatic* Library."[12] By purchasing this "complete dramatic library" in parts over a period of time, "a Subscriber may render himself master of the DRAMA of his COUNTRY, at periodical leisure, and digest its beauties with convenient deliberation." In order to make this experience and this library widely available, "the Expence, as well as the mode of publication, is adapted to different pockets and dispositions—*Elegant copies* being printed for those who prefer them, and the rest not more expensive than the very worst of other editions."

In short, Bell's advertising and packaging of literature into uniform series combined the elements of an appeal to "master" a national literary identity with the inducement of convenience and commodification, which transform volumes of verse and individual plays into a "library" of "classics." As part of this process of the commodification of literary texts, in addition to permitting one to acquire a knowledge of the nation's literature at one's convenience, at a price that would fit one's budget, and to carry one's complete national literature in attractive traveling cases (a feature continued by subsequent generations of printers and booksellers), one could also purchase other complementary items to complete one's library.

In the 4 January 1787 issue of the *World*, Bell had published a prospectus for the publication of a series of prints representing "the most interesting Subjects" from the works of "the Most Celebrated British Poets." The list of names of these celebrated individuals is worth notice. We are not surprised to find Spenser, Shakespeare, and Pope on the list; those of us who study Renaissance and Restoration texts are pleased to discover early writers represented by Sidney, Donne, and Congreve, and those who study women's texts are pleased to find Elizabeth Carter, Anna Laetitia Barbauld, Anna Seward, Hannah More, and Charlotte Smith representing the contemporary section. Scholars of any period, however, might wonder who the "celebrated" David Mallet, John Cunningham, and Mr. Pinkerton were. The answer is that they were all authors who either appeared in *Bell's British Theatre* or whose poetry he published in separate volumes; in short, they were all writers whose texts and images were already in stock, which were thus already in the machinery of production. This simple fact of copyright ownership enabled them to join the ranks of the "celebrated," not for their virtues as authors but for their cheap availability—because they were already part of the material process of filling the contents of a series.

If one compares the rhetoric of advertising associated with literary series at their emergence with that found in the late 1780s and 1790s, when the concept was firmly established, one is struck by the increasing degree to which the authors and the contents of the individual volumes have become blended into a homogeneous "library" of national literature. Whereas in the early phases of this practice Bell used the word "cheap" almost as frequently as the word "celebrated" in the proposals and prospectus for the series, after the series had been completed and existed as a unit, the group of texts as a titled series develops a new, national significance for the purchaser. In a prominent advertisement in the *Oracle* in August 1790, "the British and Irish Nations Are Respectfully intreated to become The Patrons of Fine Printing and of Beautiful Book Embellishments."[13] Bell announces that a second edition of *The British Theatre* is planned, which "will challenge the Admiration of the World." Interestingly, the "improvements," as suggested in the appeal to the British and Irish buyer, lie not in the literary content but in the increased number of engravings done by "most of the Royal Academicians" used to illustrate the plays, showing "the principle [*sic*] Performers on the London Stages . . . in their most favourite Dramatic Characters . . . in a stile of incomparable similitude."

In this same advertisement, Bell goes on to list his other offerings selected for republication, describing the advantages in purchasing literature in the periodical uniform series format. Principal among the advantages to purchasing books in series was the identification of different types of audiences with different financial situations and different cultural needs: series provide "the Inducement to Young Minds, and to Persons not accustomed to sedentary Studies, to read such Works as they wish to become acquainted with, regularly in the Process of Publication." In addition to the culturally deprived, the series provide some flexibility to the financially impoverished: "Another great Recommendation is, that the Price, thus gradually incurred, is insensibly borne, which otherwise might prove an insuperable Bar to many Persons ever being possessed of them." There is still a third class of purchasing readers, but they appear to be the smallest; Bell does say that "such Persons as object to the Progress of Periodical Publications, may have [any of the series] complete, with their appropriate Embellishments."

In the context of their republication as a complete set, *The Poets of Great Britain* are now described as "all the BRITISH CLASSICS from Chaucer to Churchill"—the "celebrated" individual has now become part of a larger phenomenon, the "BRITISH CLASSICS." By the time John Cooke has completed his series, the association of "series" with "classic" in the sense of cultural icon is firmly in place. The connection between the series format and the canon of national literature is firmly established here, since with the purchase of a series one is supposedly guaranteed "all" of the British Classics—that is, anything not in the series format is by definition not a classic British text.

On the other hand, the connection between the "classics" and the commercial is also firmly welded. This is ironic, since the implications contained in the aesthetic vocabulary used to describe and sell the volumes suggest that the texts are classic by virtue of their disengagement with the commercial, their transcendence of the present moment. In fact, their very existence in the format of a "classic" series is generated as part of the mass commodification of literary materials for a popular readership rather than for primarily aesthetic, literary considerations.

I will conclude this brief survey of the emergence of the literary series by returning to "Cooke's Pocket Edition," with which I opened, as it points towards the new "revisionary" series emerging in the late twentieth century. In the "Plan of the Pocket Library Address," Cooke explains the motives behind creating his series: "The principal motive which induced the Proprietor to submit to the public this Library, was the irregular, ponderous, and inconvenient sizes in which most of the esteemed and popular works were printed, the inelegant manner in which they were executed, and the enormous prices which have ever been attached to them" (3). The size of the volumes is one of his major sales attractions, underlining the impression of the growing connection between mass literary production and reading as a fashionable leisure activity. The small size of the volumes "forms a happy Medium between the Extremes of diminutive Inconvenience and ponderous Inutility; . . . [it] is thereby rendered as commodious for the Pocket, as it is ornamental to the book Case. Each Volume, from its convenient size, forms an agreeable Travelling Companion, adapted for Amusement at the Fire-side, and equally commodious for passing leisure Hours, when Nature and the Seasons invite us abroad" (1). When the series is at home, it provides a "UNIFORM ELEGANCE which a collection of Volumes of promiscuous sizes cannot exhibit; and the Volumes, from their uniformity, are infinitely more decorative to the Library than an arrangement in the promiscuous sizes of Quarto, Octavo, Duo-decimo, e&. This size is also more commodious than the Octavo or Duo-decimo, which are too large and ponderous for the pocket, and calculated more for works of Science than Amusement" (4).

In describing the goal of producing a series, Cooke also identifies the main markets to whom the series will appeal. His design, states Cooke, is to "gain Admission into the Cabinets of the Curious, the Libraries of the Literati, and the most fashionable of the present Age" (2). Following Bell's lead, Cooke also produced several versions of the edition with a range of prices, from the "Superior Editions" to the "Cheap" ones. The "Superior Editions" are made so because of "the distinguished Magnificence of their Embellishments, . . . adapted to accommodate the Polite and Fashionable Circles, the Virtuosos in Embellishments and the Admirers of decorative Elegance" (2). Ironically, those who chose the "Cheap Edition" must enjoy their classic texts for the literary content only, bare and unadorned, although Cooke assured the buyer that "they equal in elegance *the best of any other edition.*" Thus, the only audience for whom the classic equaled the words of the text were those who could not, or would not, invest in the deluxe, illustrated versions. For all other purchasers, "classic" included embellishment over and above the word, and its ornamental presentation signaled the status of the text and of its owner simultaneously.

Of the six paragraphs in the "Address" describing the series, four are primarily concerned with enumerating the advantages of the format and the other two in touting its cheapness. The nature of the series is neatly summed up in the declaration "As this plan has the united Advantages of ECONOMY, ELEGANCE, and PORTABILITY, it is hoped it will meet with the patronage of the Admirers of *Polite Literature.*" Although Cooke does make passing reference to the content of these volumes as comprising "all the most esteemed Works in the English language," the stress is clearly on the classic as a commodity associated with leisure entertainment and collectability rather than on a value judgment of its literary merit.

We find, for example, Shakespeare's name bracketed by Sir Richard Blackmore and James Thomson, and although Cooke declares that no poet "will gain admission into this Library but such as have been stamped with universal Approbation," the presence of playwrights David Mallet and John Cunningham on this "select" list, as well as Bell's, points, I think, less to their position as "celebrated" poets of the day than to their presence in earlier lists derived not from literary criteria but simple availability. As Richard Altick points out in his study of early-nineteenth-century series, "accessibility . . . must not be equated with popularity," and indeed many nineteenth-century series are merely reprintings of earlier ones with new titles: once an author, for whatever reason, was included in a series, he or she was likely to remain there throughout the nineteenth century. This practice, of course, had the effect of solidifying his or her reputation as a classic writer because of the continuing presence of the texts in these series; these texts, by virtue of their slot in a series, acquired "timelessness," the hallmark of a "classic."

The significance for literary historians of this new method of formatting, selling, and classifying literary texts is that it provides an excellent opportunity to reconsider the ways in which commercial decisions made in previous centuries have shaped our perception of the literary past and our own contemporary sense of what "makes" a classic. These eighteenth-century series established a way of selling literature and an aesthetic vocabulary of value that seemed to transcend the historical moment through the ties to the "classic" but which actually linked that text to the copyright constraints and the commercial possibilities of a particular period. Thus, in this example, the packaging and promotion of a series of "timeless classics" are inextricably linked with the increasing production of cheap texts, and the perception of the purchase and display of books as a type of socially accrediting leisure activity. Ironically, given the nature of these early series, almost any author thus could become a "classic" by virtue of his or her presence in this marketing format: as long as the physical nature of the volume conformed to expected standards, one doubts that Cooke, for example, paid much attention to the actual words on the page.

Today, in addition to this format of the classic reprint series, whose content is in some cases passed directly from generation to generation with the same plates, we have the advent of a new type of uniform series and new technologies to generate its contents. The "revisionary" series, unlike the reprint series, does not rely on previous generations of editors' choices of texts or authors but instead must create its own list. Unlike these eighteenth- and nineteenth-century examples of series in which the content was significantly affected by copyright law and by the commercial practice of purchasing preexisting series plates, there are several new series that cannot rely on the judgment or economic determinants that shaped earlier lists. Series such as the Schomberg Library of Nineteenth-Century Black Women Writers, edited by Henry Louis Gates Jr.; the Early American Womens Writers Series, edited by Cathy N. Davidson; and the Women Writers in English 1350–1850 Series, edited by Susanne Woods and Elizabeth Hageman, are concerned with recovering writings by women and ethnic minorities, writers absent from the nineteenth- and early-twentieth-century lists.

This new type of uniform series raises critical issues for our consideration concerning the historical nature of the politics of aesthetics. Why were these texts not included in the earlier reprint series, whose lists, as we have seen, certainly carried along the names of many male writers no longer ranked among the classics? In considering the new series themselves, we face two types of questions: what "makes" a text by a nontraditional writer previously excluded from the designation into a "classic," a text worthy to be placed in an institutional context such as a series? Second, does this new type of series need to continue the historically based practice of seeking out "classic" texts, however they are defined, after the pattern established to commodify and institutionalize British male authors, or should a new criterion of "classic" be involved for this new type of series?

John Cooke's Pocket Editions in the eighteenth and nineteenth centuries announced that they would establish the genius of British writers to the wonderment of other nations, for all times. In doing so, Cooke's series was making the claim for the value and significance of literature in English as ranking with that of the established, institutional Greek and Roman classics. Even though their contents offer a radical challenge to the assumptions imbedded in the old reprint series, the editors and publishers of these new revisionary series and new types of publishing ventures are continuing this pattern of changing the perceptions of literary life in the past and questioning existing models of literary history.

Postscript

In considering the preceding essays, which looked at the specific material conditions of authorship in the period leading up to modern practices and the establishment of copyright, larger issues obviously arise about writing, reading, and the nature of literary history. Addressing these issues is beyond the scope of this volume, but they do suggest fruitful possibilities for future exploration.

For example, if we accept the notion that there was a class of writers and readers for whom print and general commercial readership were neither the goal nor the norm, we need to consider how that affects our reading of the texts they produced, often as collaborative projects. Likewise, if we challenge the narrative of the triumph of print occurring during the Civil War years and also accept the possibility of an inevitable time lapse between the availability of a technology and its widespread use and application, we may find that there are other stories of the book and its relationship with print, of the relationships between author and reader.

If we also consider that the institutionalization of laws governing literature as property and the older notion of the text as a dynamic and collaborative process appear to have coexisted well into the mid-eighteenth century, our description of what constitutes being an author must reflect the continued presence of the social writer and his or her audiences. The question must be asked, what happens to our perception of texts and writers who participated in both practices, such as Pope? Moreover, in considering the emergence of the marketing of literary series, with their emphasis on creating a "national" author as a commodity for readers to collect, we seem to see in process the replacement of the "social" author and manuscript practice, which involved the active participation of both writer and reader in sustaining a dynamic of literary culture, by that of the marketing agent and the passive purchaser. This can be seen as a shift from the role of the reader as participating in creating and producing literary texts, as seen, for example, in the Aston and North families, to the reader as anonymous consumer and collector, as characterized by the purchasers of Bell's and Cooke's series.

Finally, given our own contemporary confrontation with new modes of authorship, we are facing a new but still familiar set of questions about authors, readers, and the production of texts. Proponents of electronic publication, on the one hand, say that they offer "author empowerment" by liberating the writer from the constraints and expenses of publication; on the other hand, others deride the same technology for creating an undisciplined environment favoring the potential erosion of professional standards. Proponents celebrate the fluid, interactive nature of the textual medium; sceptics lament the confusion of authorial proprieties and unauthorized use of others' words and work. What can we learn from early culture of authorship that is relevant to our current situation? Are we returning to the early modern model of manuscript text and social authorship, or are we positioned to invent yet another story to add to this tale?

NOTES

Introduction
The Changing Culture of Authorship
and the History of the Book

1. François Furet, *In the Workshop of History,* trans. Jonathan Mandelbaum (Chicago: Univ. of Chicago Press, 1984), 99.

2. See, for example, Mark Rose's recent study *Authors and Owners: The Invention of Copyright* (Cambridge: Harvard Univ. Press, 1993). This monograph is the latest of a series of investigations of the notion of "intellectual property" in general and in particular the economic conditions of authorship in early modern England: see early classic studies by Leo Kirschbaum, "Author's Copyright in England before 1640," *Publications of the Bibliographical Society of America* 40 (1946): 43–80, and Edward Bloom, "Samuel Johnson on Copyright," *Journal of English and German Philology* 47 (1948): 165–72; Terry Belanger, "Publishers and Writers in Eighteenth-Century England," in *Books and Their Readers in Eighteenth-Century England,* ed. Isabel Rivers (London: St. Martin's Press, 1982), 5–25; Joseph Loewenstein, "For a History of Literary Property: John Wolfe's Reformation," *English Literary Renaissance* 18 (1988): 389–412, and "The Script in the Marketplace," *Representations* 12 (1985): 101–14; Martha Woodmansee, "The Genius and the Copyright: Economic and Legal Conditions of the Emergence of the 'Author,'" *Eighteenth-Century Studies* 17 (1984): 425–48; David Saunders and Ian Hunter, "Lessons from the 'Literatory': How to Historicize Authorship," *Critical Inquiry* 17 (1991): 479–509; Dustin Griffin, "Fictions of Eighteenth-Century Authorship," *Essays in Criticism* 43 (1993): 181–94, and Pamela O. Long, "Invention, Authorship, 'Intellectual Property,' and the Origin of Patents: Notes toward a Conceptual History," *Technology and Culture* 32 (1991): 846–84.

3. For an overview of this group of texts, see Roger Chartier, *The Order of Books,* trans. Lydia G. Cochrane (Stanford: Stanford Univ. Press, 1994), especially chap. 2.

4. Elizabeth Eisenstein, *The Printing Press an an Agent of Change* (Cambridge: Cambridge Univ. Press, 1980), 121.

5. In *Is Literary History Possible?* (Baltimore: Johns Hopkins Univ. Press, 1992), David Perkins objects to studies of texts that he terms "literary sociology," which he feels "are of not much interest [to] literary readers" (177).

6. For an interesting analysis of the ways in which electronic authorship is being constructed and perhaps misconceptualized, see Richard Grusin, "What Is an Electronic Author? Theory and the Technological Fallacy," *Configurations* 3 (1994): 469–83. Grusin argues that the "logic of authorship" presented by key recent studies on electronic authorship—Mark Poster, *The Mode of Information: Poststructuralism and Social Context* (Chicago: Univ. of Chicago Press, 1990); Jay David Bolter, *Writing Space: The Computer, Hypertext, and the History of Writing* (Hillsdale, N.J.: L. Erlbaum Associates, 1991); George Landow, *Hypertext: The Convergence of Contemporary Critical Theory and Technology* (Baltimore: Johns Hopkins Univ. Press, 1992); and Richard Lanham, *The Electronic Word: Democracy, Technology, and the Arts* (Chicago: Univ. of Chicago Press, 1993)—is based on what he calls a "technological fallacy" that "ascribe[s] agency to technology itself, [using] statements in which the technologies of electronic writing are described as actors" (470). In Grusin's view, while such studies posit that electronic publishing "instantiate[s] the theoretical assertions of poststructuralism, postmodernism, or deconstruction," they do so by "elid[ing] or marginaliz[ing] the materiality of these technologies" (471). See also studies such as that by Stephen Marcus, "Reading, Writing, and Hypertext," *College Literature* 15 (1988), which is concerned about "the manner in which computer technology is changing the nature of the product as well as the process of decoding and encoding what is on our minds" (9).

7. Gary Taubes, "Electronic Preprints Point the Way to 'Author Empowerment,'" *Science* 271 (1996): 767–68, and subsequent discussions of its practicalities and problems in letters from various journal editors and Internet users, "Electronic Publishing," *Science* 272 (1996): 15–17.

8. As early as 1985, Stanford University's president, Donald Kennedy, called for the development of a new "protocol for accepting or assigning authorship of scientific articles" because of concerns over multiauthor pieces; the addition of issues raised by electronic publishing has yet to be addressed systematically by the profession. Barbara J. Culliton, "Stanford President Calls for New Authorship Policy," *Science* 230 (1985): 422–23.

9. Christopher Small, *The Printed Word: An Instrument of Popularity* (Aberdeen, Scotland: Aberdeen Univ. Press, 1982), 23.

10. Nigel Smith, *Literature and Revolution in England, 1640–1660* (New Haven: Yale Univ. Press, 1994); Margaret Spufford, *Small Books and Pleasant Histories* (Athens: Univ. of Georgia Press, 1981); see also Jerome Friedman, *The Battle of the Frogs and Fairford's Flies: Miracles and the Pulp Press during the English Revolution* (New York: St. Martin's Press, 1993); Sharon Achinstein, *Milton and the Revolution-*

ary Reader (Princeton: Princeton Univ. Press, 1994). For the debate over literacy rates and standards, see Spufford's rebuttal of David Cressy's study in her article "First Steps in Literacy: The Reading and Writing Experiences of the Humblest Seventeenth-Century Spiritual Autobiographers," *Social History* 4 (1979): 407–35, and also Cressy's response, "Literacy in Context: Meaning and Measurements in Early Modern England," in *Consumption and the World of Goods,* ed. John Brewer and Roy Porter (London: Routledge, 1993), 305–19. Sara Heller Mendelson, "Stuart Women's Diaries," in *Women in English Society, 1500–1800,* ed. Mary Prior (London: Methuen, 1985), has a useful analysis of how gender factors skew Cressy's results. See also Keith Thomas, "The Meaning of Literacy in Early Modern England," in *The Written Word: Literacy in Transition,* ed. Gerd Bauman (Oxford: Oxford Univ. Press, 1986).

11. Joshua Lerner, "Science and Agricultural Progress: Quantitative Evidence from England, 1660–1780," *Agricultural History* 66 (1992): 14, 21.

12. See, for example, the recent study by Kevin Pask, *The Emergence of the English Author: Scripting the Life of the Poet in Early Modern England* (Cambridge: Cambridge Univ. Press, 1996), which focuses on Chaucer, Sidney, Spenser, Donne, and Milton, looking at contemporary "lives of the poets" to trace "the emergence of the poet's life through its imbrication with early genres of life-writing" and the creation of a "professional" author in such texts (5).

13. Julie Stone Peters, *Congreve, the Drama, and the Printed Word* (Stanford: Stanford Univ. Press, 1990), 15, 17.

14. Alvin Kernan, *Samuel Johnson and the Impact of Print* (Princeton: Princeton Univ. Press, 1987), 4, 5.

15. Eisenstein, *Printing Press as an Agent of Change,* 121.

16. Evelyn B. Tribble, *Margins and Marginality: The Printed Page in Early Modern England* (Charlottesville: Univ. Press of Virginia, 1993).

17. John Kerrigan, "The Editor as Reader," in *The Practice and Representation of Reading in England,* ed. James Raven, Helen Small, and Naomi Tadmor (Cambridge: Cambridge Univ. Press, 1996), 120. Gerald MacLean investigates the connection between the government, the press, and the reading audience in "Literacy, Class, and Gender in Restoration England," *Text* 7 (1995): 307–35. For a study of the development of reading audiences in the later part of the eighteenth century, see Jon P. Klancher, *The Making of English Reading Audiences, 1790–1832* (Madison: Univ. of Wisconsin Press, 1987), and Barbara Benedict, *Making the Modern Reader: Cultural Mediation in Early Modern Literary Anthologies* (Princeton: Princeton Univ. Press, 1996).

18. Adam Fox, in "Popular Verses and Their Readership in the Early Seventeenth Century," in Raven, Small, and Tadmor, *Practice and Representation of Reading in England,* does mention that "hand-written publications were not necessarily any less widely disseminated than pieces of cheap print" (128), but since his concern is

in examining the relationship between oral culture and reading practices, this point is not pursued. Likewise, MacLean's interest lies in investigating the role of printed text and its producers in shaping political events.

19. A fascinating exception to this is found in Nancy Pollard Brown's study of the transmission of forbidden Catholic texts in early-seventeenth-century England through the circulation of manuscript volumes, "Paperchase: The Dissemination of Catholic Texts in Elizabethan England," *English Manuscript Studies, 1100–1700* 1 (1989): 120–43.

20. Marjorie Plant, *The English Book Trade: An Economic History of the Making and Sale of Books*, 3d ed. (London: George Allen & Unwin, 1974), 23.

21. See Plant, *English Book Trade*; Friedman, *Battle of the Frogs*; and Smith, *Literature and Revolution*, for detailed analyses.

22. See Perkins, *Is Literary History Possible?*, for an overview of traditional modes of literary history and their relationship with formalism.

23. Jonathan Rose, "Rereading the English Common Reader: A Preface to a History of Audiences," *Journal of the History of Ideas* 53 (1992): 47.

24. David Hall, quoted in ibid., 47.

25. G. Thomas Tanselle, "Printing History and Other History," *Studies in Bibliography* 48 (1995): 271.

26. Michel Foucault, "What Is an Author?" in *Critical Theory since 1965*, ed. Hazard Adams and Leroy Searle (Tallahassee: Univ. of Florida Press, 1992), 142.

27. See Harry Ransom, *The First Copyright Statute* (Austin: Univ. of Texas Press, 1956).

28. Henri-Jean Martin, *The History and Power of Writing*, trans. Lydia G. Cochrane (Chicago: Univ. of Chicago Press, 1994), 233. See his chap. 6, "The Reign of the Book," for further discussion.

29. Harold Love, *Scribal Publication in Seventeenth-Century England* (London: Oxford Univ. Press, 1993), 3, 9.

30. Bonamy Dobrée, *English Literature in the Early Eighteenth Century, 1700–1740* (Oxford: Clarendon Press, 1959), and Hippolyte Taine, *History of English Literature*, trans. N. Van Laun (New York: William L. Allison Co., 1895).

31. James Sutherland, *English Literature of the Late Seventeenth Century* (Oxford: Clarendon Press, 1969), and C. V. Wedgwood, *Seventeenth-Century English Literature* (New York: Oxford Univ. Press, 1950).

Chapter One
The Social Author

1. Mary Hobbs, "Early Seventeenth-Century Verse Miscellanies and Their Value for Textual Editors," *English Manuscript Studies, 1100–1700* 1 (1989): 182–210. Like most commentators, Hobbs notes that "the peak period of manuscript verse miscel-

lanies seems, for some reason, to have been the 1630s," but in contrast to editorial tradition, she offers a strong argument for the use of manuscript miscellanies rather than relying solely on printed texts in creating scholarly editions (200).

2. For views on authors who did not desire to be published, see Margaret J. M. Ezell, *The Patriarch's Wife: Literary Evidence and the History of the Family* (Chapel Hill: Univ. of North Carolina Press, 1987), chap. 3. For earlier periods, the classic study is J. W. Sanders, "The Stigma of Print: A Note on the Social Bases of Tudor Poetry," *Essays in Criticism* 1 (1951): 139–64. This original theory of the social importance of avoiding print for the group Sanders identifies as the "Courtier" poets has been challenged by Steven W. May, "Tudor Aristocrats and the Mythical 'Stigma of Print," *Renaissance Papers* 10 (1980): 11–18, who finds that the theory of the supposed "social code" obliging aristocrats to shun the press, "handy and time-honoured as it has become, does not square with the evidence" (11). May further explores the role of poetry in Elizabeth's court in his most recent study, *The Elizabethan Courtier Poets: The Poems and Their Contexts* (Columbia: Univ. of Missouri Press, 1991).

3. As note 2 suggests, the latter part of the sixteenth and the earlier seventeenth centuries have had much more scholarly attention directed to the phenomenon of scribal verse circulation; any editor of John Donne or Sir Philip Sidney, for example, must deal with the complexities posed by the circulation of his work in manuscript. For discussions of manuscript authorship during this period, see Arthur F. Marotti, *Manuscript, Print, and the English Renaissance Lyric* (Ithaca, N.Y.: Cornell Univ. Press, 1995), in which he observes that while the 1620s and 1630s have been called "the golden age of MS verse compilation" by critics, "many large collections, in fact, were assembled though the 1640s, 1650s, and into the Restoration period," although he believes that "the re-establishment of the monarchy significantly changed the sociopolitical context of manuscript transmission and compilation and the number of such collections dropped markedly" (68–60). See also Wendy Wall, *The Imprint of Gender: Authorship and Publication in the English Renaissance* (Ithaca, N.Y.: Cornell Univ. Press, 1993), which is specifically interested in the development of a concept of authorship as masculine, which emerged through social controversies over print and the "specific genres, strategies, and gestures through which that gendering occurred" (3–4). For studies focused on a particular author's literary experiences, see Richard B. Wollman, "The 'Press and the Fire': Print and MSS Culture in Donne's Circle," *Studies in English Literature, 1599–1900* 33 (1993): 85–97; Alan MacColl, "The Circulation of Donne's Poems in Manuscript" in *John Donne: Essays in Celebration*, ed. A. J. Smith (London: Methuen: 1972), 28–46; Katherine Duncan-Jones' detailed study of Sidney, *Sir Philip Sidney: Life, Death, and Legend* (Oxford: Clarendon Press, 1986), and, more recently, *Sir Philip Sidney: Courtier Poet* (New Haven: Yale Univ. Press, 1991), along with H. R. Woudhuysen's excellent

study of Sir Philip Sidney's participation in manuscript circulation and of the professional scribes who created the manuscript copies in *Sir Philip Sidney and the Circulation of Manuscripts, 1558–1640* (Oxford: Clarendon Press, 1996). As this essay shows, I am indebted to both Marotti and Woudhuysen but disagree on the nature of manuscript circulation and on its seeming rate of decline.

4. In 1997, the Perdita Project was established by Nottingham Trent University; its goal is to compile a database, to be published on the Internet, of early modern women's manuscript texts.

5. Brice Harris, "Captain Robert Julian, Secretary to the Muses," *ELH* 10 (1943): 294.

6. David Vieth, *Attribution in Restoration Poetry* (New Haven: Yale Univ. Press, 1963), 23–24. The definition of terms found in the first volume of the *Index of English Literary Manuscripts*, ed. Peter Beal (New York: Bowker, 1980–), is also useful for making the distinction between manuscript miscellanies and commonplace books. See also Peter Beal's comments in "Notations in Garrison: The Seventeenth-Century Commonplace Book," in *New Ways of Looking at Old Texts*, ed. W. Speed Hill (Binghamton, N.Y.: Renaissance Text Society, 1993): 131–47.

7. Arthur Clifford, ed., *Tixall Poetry* (Edinburgh, 1813), xxvii. For a detailed analysis of the family connections, see Victoria Elizabeth Burke, "Women and Seventeenth-Century Manuscript Culture: Miscellanies, Commonplace Books, and Song Books Compiled by English and Scottish Women, 1600–1660" (Ph.D. diss., Oxford University, 1996), and Jenijoy LaBelle, "The Huntington Aston Manuscript," *Book Collector* 29 (1980): 542–67, and "A True Love's Knot: The Letters of Constance Fowler and the Poems of Herbert Aston," *Journal of English and Germanic Philology* 79 (1980): 13–31.

8. Beinicke Library, Yale University, Osborne MS b.4; Huntington Library, HM 904.

9. Arthur Clifford, ed., *Tixall Letters,* 2 vols. (Edinburgh, 1815), 2:133.

10. See also Victoria Burke, "Women and Early Seventeenth-Century Manuscript Culture: Four Miscellanies," *Seventeenth Century* 12 (1997): 135–50, for discussion of Fowler's labors.

11. *The Poems of Patrick Cary,* ed. Sister Veronica Delaney (Oxford: Clarendon Press, 1978), 4, 41.

12. This same type of Royalist audience for literary manuscript materials during the Interregnum is also demonstrated in the manuscript volume compiled by the daughters of the duke of Newcastle, Lady Elizabeth Brackley and Jane Cavendish, which I discuss in "'To Be Your Daughter in Your Pen': The Social Functions of Literature in the Writings of Lady Elizabeth Brackley and Lady Jane Cavendish," *Huntington Library Quarterly* 51 (1988): 281–96.

13. Bodleian Library, MS Rawl.poet.87, 13.

14. For example, "Of that poore might we humbly come to pay" is corrected to "mite" by the use of a strikethrough line (2), and "Phyloclea" is overwritten to become "Phíloclea"; and in the poem on Lady Victoria Uvedale, the writer originally penned the line as "Call in his beames, a soon's his race is run" but then struck through "a soon's," replacing it with the simpler "when" and adding "swift" before "race." Bodleian Library, MS Rawl.poet.87, 2, 13.

15. Peter Giles, "An Unknown Emmanuel Poet," *Emmanuel College Magazine* 9 (1897): 2.

16. Bodleian Library, MS Rawl.poet.94.

17. Cole was a staunch Royalist, who was proposed for one of Charles II' s new orders of knighthood, the "Knights of the Royal Oak," an honor that Chatwin celebrates in a poem in the volume. For further details concerning Cole, see John Nichols, *The History and Antiquities of the County of Leicester,* 2d ed. (London, 1813), 4:272.

18. This was Heneage Finch, the second son of the earl of Nottingham and himself the future earl of Aylesford. For information about Burroughs, see Giles, "Unknown Emmanuel Poet," 2–4; for information about Finch, see Nichols, *History and Antiquities,* 2:17.

19. Wanley's poem is found in British Library MSS Harleian 6646 and 6922. L. C. Martin, "A Forgotten Poet of the Seventeenth Century," *Essays and Studies* 11 (1925): 5–31; see also Martin's 1928 Oxford edition of Wanley's verse.

20. Bodleian Library, MS Rawl.poet.208.

21. Joseph Foster, *Alumni Oxonienses: The Members of the University of Oxford, 1500–1714* (1891; reprint, Nendeln, Liechtenstein: Kraus Reprint, 1968), 2:742. The other possibility among Oxford students would be Joseph Hooper, also of Devon, admitted to Wadham College, 23 May 1667, age seventeen.

22. Dale B. J. Randall, *Gentle Flame: The Life and Verse of Dudley, Fourth Lord North (1602–1677)* (Durham, N.C.: Duke Univ. Press, 1983), 100–101.

23. St. John's College, MS bb, James 613, vol. 1, p. [41]; quoted in Randall, *Gentle Flame,* 106.

24. Marotti, *Manuscript, Print, and the English Renaissance Lyric,* 68–69; Woudhuysen, *Sir Philip Sidney,* 391.

25. Cary's anti-Crowmell verses were in fact mild compared with those of Thomas Weaver, who compiled a manuscript volume of verse (Bodleian Library, MS Rawl.poet.211), which among other pieces contained dated "Carols" for Christmas attacking the government. Some of the contents of this manuscript text were published in 1654 as *Songs and Poems of Love and Drollery,* by "T.W."

26. Burghope, CH EL/35/B/62.

27. For a more extended discussion of this, see Ezell, "'To Be Your Daughter in Your Pen'"; for a later example, see Katherine King's analysis of Jane Barker's texts in

"Jane Barker, *Poetical Recreations,* and the Sociable Text," *ELH* 61 (1994): 551–70.

28. Angeline Goreau, *Reconstructing Aphra: A Social Biography of Aphra Behn* (Oxford: Clarendon Press, 1980), 153–54.

29. Earl Miner, *The Cavalier Modes from Jonson to Cotton* (Princeton: Princeton Univ. Press, 1971), 275.

30. King, "Jane Barker." See also Kathryn R. King and Jeslyn Medoff's recent bio-bibliographical study of Barker for further information concerning the author's practices in exile in France in "Jane Barker and Her Life (1652–1732): The Documentary Record," *Eighteenth-Century Life* 21 (1997): 16–38.

31. Marie Burghope's text, for example, survived because it was part of the Huntington family library and was bought as part of a collection of that family's papers.

32. Sir John Clerk, *Memoirs of the Life of Sir John Clerk of Penicuik, Baronet,* ed. John M. Gay (Edinburgh, 1892), 10.

33. Mary Mollineux, *Fruits of Retirement* (London, 1702).

34. For statistics on Quaker women writers publishing during the close of the seventeenth century, see Margaret J. M. Ezell, *Writing Women's Literary History* (Baltimore: Johns Hopkins Univ. Press, 1993), chap. 5.

35. "The Early Seventeenth Century," in *The Norton Anthology of English Literature,* 6th ed. (New York: Norton, 1993), 1:1079.

Chapter Two
Literary Pirates and Reluctant Authors

1. Ursula Quarles, preface to Francis Quarles, *Judgment and Mercie for Afflicted Souls* (London, 1646).

2. Richard Marriott and Henry Herringman, "To the Writer," in Henry King, *Poems, Elegies* (London, 1657).

3. See, for example, H. P. Bennett's study of the early seventeenth century, *English Books and Readers, 1603 to 1640* (Cambridge: Cambridge Univ. Press, 1970), 65.

4. Quoted in Elizabeth Hageman, "Making a Good Impression: Early Texts and Letters by Katherine Philips," *South Central Review* 11 (1994): 47.

5. Cotton Mather, *MS. Life,* quoted in Elizabeth Wade White, *Anne Bradstreet: "The Tenth Muse"* (New York: Oxford Univ. Press, 1971), 179.

6. "As weary pilgrim, now at rest" was first printed in 1867 in J. H. Ellis's edition of *The Works of Anne Bradstreet* (White, *Anne Bradstreet,* 354). For accounts of the dating of her poems, see, in addition to White, Rosamond Rosenmeier, *Anne Bradstreet Revisited* (Boston: Twayne Publishers, 1991).

7. Rosenmeier, *Bradstreet Revisited,* 131–32; see Adelaide P. Amore, *A Woman's Inner World: Selected Prose and Poetry of Anne Bradstreet* (Lanham, Md.: Univ. Press of America, 1982), xvii, for references to "family" readings.

8. For a discussion of the identity of the editor of *Several Poems,* see White's ac-

count of Jeannine Hensley's analysis of this volume, in *Anne Bradstreet*, 362–64.

9. Henry Lawes, "To All Understanders or Lovers of Music," *Ayres and Dialogues* (1653), quoted in Willa McClung Evans, *Henry Lawes: Musician and Friend of Poets* (New York: Modern Language Association, 1941), 198.

10. Ezell, *Patriarch's Wife*, 85–87. For alternative views, see Patrick Thomas's introduction to Katherine Philips, *The Collected Works of Katherine Philips, the Matchless Orinda*, ed. Patrick Thomas, 3 vols. (Essex: Stump Cross Press, 1990); Claudia A. Limbert, "Katherine Philips: Controlling a Life and Reputation," *South Atlantic Review* 56 (1991): 27–42; Catherine Cole Mambretti, "Fugitive Papers: A New Orinda Poem and Problems in Her Canon," *Publications of the Bibliographical Society of America* 71 (1977): 443–52; Dorothy Mermin, "Women Becoming Poets: Katherine Philips, Anne Finch, Aphra Behn," *ELH* 57 (1990): 335–55; Harriette Andreadis, "The Sapphic-Platonics of Katherine Philips, 1632–1664," *Signs* 15 (1989): 34–60.

11. Katherine Philips, *Letters from Orinda to Poliarchus* (London, 1705), 228.

12. Elizabeth Hageman and Andrea Sununu, "New Manuscript Texts of Katherine Philips, the Matchless Orinda," in *English Manuscript Studies, 1100–1700* 4 (1993): 214.

13. Jane Barker, *The Galesia Trilogy and Selected Manuscript Poems*, ed. Carol Shiner Wilson (New York: Oxford Univ. Press, 1997), xxiv. Kathryn R. King, in her study of the volume, clears up the dating of it: although 1688 is the date on the title page, the volume itself physically appeared 1687. King, "Jane Barker," 552.

14. King, "Jane Barker," 559. The relationship between Barker and Crayle has some resemblance to that a decade later between the publisher John Dunton and Elizabeth Singer Rowe, his "Pindaric Lady," whose occasional verse he printed but who strenuously objected to having her works collected in a volume.

15. Magdalen College, Oxford, Magdalen MS 343, pt. 3, headnote. I am indebted to Carol Shiner Wilson for this citation.

16. Nathan P. Tinker, "John Grismond: Printer of the Unauthorized Edition of Katherine Philips's *Poems* (1664)," *English Language Notes* 34 (1996): 30–31.

17. See Hageman, "Making a Good Impression," 49, for a discussion of these events.

18. John Dunton, *The Life and Errors of John Dunton . . . to which are added Selections from his Other Genuine Works* (1818; reprint, New York: Burt Franklin, 1969), 1:154. For further information on Dunton and the *Spira* text, see Stephen Parks, *John Dunton and the English Book Trade: A Study of His Career with a Checklist of His Publications* (New York: Garland Publishing, 1976), 57–59.

19. R. R. Bowker, *Copyright: Its History and Law* (Boston: Houghton Mifflin, 1912), 251, quoted in Cyril Bathurst Judge, *Elizabethan Book Pirates* (Cambridge: Harvard Univ. Press, 1934), 29.

20. Robert W. Uphaus and Gretchen M. Foster, eds., *The Other Eighteenth Century: English Women of Letters, 1660–1800* (East Lansing, Mich.: Colleagues Press, 1991), 151.

21. Jerome McGann, "The Text, the Poem, and the Problem of Historical Method," in *The Beauty of Inflections: Literary Investigations in Historical Method and Theory* (Oxford: Clarendon Press, 1985): 111–32.

22. In addition to the critical studies of earlier seventeenth-century manuscript cultures mentioned above, see also Peter Beal's introduction to the *Index of English Literary Manuscripts*, a project of immense scope and value in reconstructing earlier periods' literary practices.

Chapter Three
The Very Early Career of Alexander Pope

1. Harry Ransom, "The Rewards of Authorship in the Eighteenth Century," *University of Texas Studies in English* 18 (1938): 51.

2. Maynard Mack, *Alexander Pope: A Life* (New York: Norton, 1985), 110.

3. John Butt, "Pope's Poetical Manuscripts," in *Essential Articles for the Study of Alexander Pope*, ed. Maynard Mack, rev. ed. (Hamden, Conn.: Archon Books, 1968), 545.

4. The classic studies of Pope's texts include Butt, "Pope's Poetical Manuscripts"; George Sherburn, *The Early Career of Alexander Pope* (Oxford: Clarendon Press, 1934); and Norman Ault, *New Light on Pope with Some Additions to His Poetry Hitherto Unknown* (London: Methuen, 1949).

5. David Foxon, *Pope and the Early Eighteenth-Century Book Trade*, rev. ed. by James McLaverty (Oxford: Clarendon Press, 1991); Pat Rogers, *Grub Street: Studies in a Subculture* (London: Methuen, 1972).

6. See James A. Winn, *A Window in the Bosom* (Hamden, Conn.: Archon Books, 1977), chap. 1; James McLaverty, "The First Printing and Publication of Pope's Letters," *Library* 2 (1980): 264–80; Rosemary Cowler's introductions in volume 2 of *The Prose Works of Alexander Pope* (Hamden, Conn.: Archon Books, 1986) also contain excellent accounts of the actions and issues surrounding the publication of the letters and Pope's participation in it.

7. Pat Rogers, "Pope and His Subscribers," *Publishing History* 3 (1978): 7–36.

8. Sherburn, *Early Career*. For example, Sherburn gives one chapter to "Family and Childhood" and another to "Making Friends, 1705–15."

9. Joseph Spence, *Anecdotes, Observations, and Characters of Books and Men*, ed. Samuel Weller Singer, intro. Bonamy Dobrée (1819; reprint, Carbondale: Southern Illinois Press, 1964), 169.

10. James A. Winn, "On Pope, Printers, and Publishers," *Eighteenth-Century Life* 6 (1981): 98, 99.

11. See, for example, Cowler's description of the "engineering" of the publication

in *Prose Works*, 2:319, 348 n. 17, and her account of Whitwell Elwin's view of Pope's moral turpitude in his early edition of Pope's works (319).

12. Howard Erskine-Hill, "Alexander Pope at Fifteen: A New Manuscript," *Review of English Studies*, n.s., 18 (1966): 277.

13. See, in particular, Rogers, *Grub Street*.

14. Alexander Pope, *The Correspondence,* ed. George Sherburn (Oxford: Clarendon Press, 1956), 1:50. It is also of interest that in the 1699 *Dictionary of Cant*, "hacks," in addition to being defined as "Poor Hirelings Mercenary Writers," are first defined as being "Hackney-whores, Common Prostitutes." See Kathy Mac-Dermott, "Literature and the Grub Street Myth," *Literature and History* 8 (1982): 159–69.

15. 20 May 1709, *Correspondence*, 1:60–61.

16. Foxon, *Book Trade*, 15–16; *Tatler*, 12 April 1709.

17. Phyllis Freeman, "Two Fragments of Walsh Manuscripts," *Review of English Studies*, n.s., 8 (1957): 390.

18. Kari Michelle Kraus, "The Wit Restor'd; or, The Critics' Rejoinder: A Revaluation of William Walsh" (M.A. thesis, Texas A&M University, 1995), 24.

19. John Dryden, *The Letters of John Dryden,* ed. Charles E. Ward (Durham, N.C.: Duke Univ. Press, 1942), 32.

20. See Kraus, "Wit Restor'd," 25–26, and Phyllis Freeman, "William Walsh and Dryden: Recently Recovered Letters," *Review of English Studies* 24 (1948): 195–202.

21. Walsh's manuscripts are found in Bodleian MS Malone 9 and British Library MSS Add. 10434 and Harleian 7001.

22. Lady Mary Wortley Montagu, *The Complete Letters,* ed. Robert Halsband (Oxford: Clarendon Press, 1965–67), 1:309–402.

23. Isobel Grundy, "The Politics of Female Authorship: Lady Mary Wortley Montagu's Reaction to the Printing of her Poems," *Book Collector* 31 (1982): 19.

24. Ralph Straus, *The Unspeakable Curll: Being Some Account of the Life of Edmund Curll, Bookseller* (London: Chapman and Hall, 1927), 49.

25. Quoted in ibid., 53; see also Robert Halsband, "Pope, Lady Mary, and the Court Poems," *PMLA* 68 (1953): 237–50, and Halsband, *The Life of Lady Mary Wortley Montagu* (London: Oxford Univ. Press, 1956), 53–54.

26. See Foxon, *Book Trade*, chap. 2.

27. Ibid., table 4, "Pope's Publications, 1709–1720," 40–41. See also Ian Watt, "Publishers and Sinners: The Augustan View," *Studies in Bibliography* 12 (1958): 3–20.

28. For an interesting account of communication networks among Catholic families in the late sixteenth and earlier seventeenth centuries, see Brown, "Paperchase," 120–43, and John Bossy, *The English Catholic Community, 1579–1850* (London: Darton, 1975).

29. Alexander Pope, *The Prose Works of Alexander Pope,* ed. Norman Ault (Oxford: Basil Blackwell, 1936), 1:171.

30. Howard Erskine-Hill, "Under Which Caesar? Pope in the Journal of Mrs. Charles Caesar," *Review of English Studies,* n.s., 33 (1982): 436–44.

31. See, in addition to Erskine-Hill's article on Mrs. Caesar, Rogers, "Pope and His Subscribers."

32. The scrapbook is held at Trinity College, Cambridge, Wren Library, B.4.13.

33. Thomas Jackson, ed. "The Life of Elizabeth Singer Rowe," in *Library of Christian Biography* (London, 1839), 10:196.

Chapter Four

Getting into Print

1. For an account of the procedures for what Harold Love terms "scribal publication," or the hiring of professional copyists to create multiple manuscript texts resembling printed ones, see his exhaustive account in *Scribal Publication.* For the issues I am addressing, I have preferred to avoid this term, since for the range of manuscript practices we find in this period it again implies that the mode and motive of writing were the same as for print, to achieve a public audience, only with a different type of ink.

2. Plant, *English Book Trade,* 83–84. For further information concerning the number and location of printing presses in England before 1660 and the specific ordinances and decrees that affected them, see W. W. Greg, *Some Aspects and Problems of London Publishing between 1550 and 1650* (Oxford: Clarendon Press, 1956); Cyprian Blagden, *The Stationers Company: A History, 1403–1959* (Cambridge: Harvard Univ. Press, 1960); Leona Rostenberg, *Literary, Political, Scientific, Religious, and Legal Publishing, Printing, and Bookselling in England, 1551–1700: Twelve Studies* (New York: Burt Franklin, 1965), vol. 1; P. M. Handover, *Printing in London from 1476 to Modern Times* (Cambridge: Harvard Univ. Press, 1960); and Bennett, *English Books and Readers.*

3. M. Pollard, *Dublin's Trade in Books, 1550–1800* (Oxford: Clarendon Press, 1989), 8, 2–4.

4. John Feather, *The Provincial Book Trade in Eighteenth-Century England* (Cambridge: Cambridge Univ. Press, 1985), 2.

5. Richard Waller to Sir Robert Sibbold, Royal Society Manuscript, LBC.11.(1), 250.

6. Richard Waller to Hans Sloane, British Library Manuscript, Sloane 4061, f. 257.

7. Margaret J. M. Ezell, "The *Gentleman's Journal* and the Commercialization of Restoration Coterie Literary Practices," *Modern Philology* 89 (1992): 323–40.

8. Arise Evans, *A Voice from Heaven* (London, 1652), "To the Reader," sig. A2r.

9. Quoted in Kathleen Lynch, *Jacob Tonson, Kit-Cat Publisher* (Knoxville: Univ. of Tennessee Press, 1971), 99–100.

10. Dryden, *Letters*; see also James Winn, *John Dryden and His World* (New Haven: Yale Univ. Press, 1987), for an account of Dryden's financial difficulties and his arrangements with his lifelong printer Jacob Tonson, especially 474–84; see also Charles E. Ward, "The Publication and Profits of Dryden's *Virgil*," *PMLA* 53 (1938): 807–12.

11. For investigations concerning the development and continuing debate over the nature of English copyright throughout the eighteenth century, see Jeremy Black, *The English Press in the Eighteenth Century* (Philadelphia: Univ. of Pennsylvania Press, 1987); Edward Bloom, "Samuel Johnson on Copyright," *Journal of English and German Philology* 47 (1948): 165–72; Leo Kirschbaum, "Authors' Copyright in England before 1640," *Publications of the Bibliographical Society of America* 40 (1946): 43–80; Joseph Loewenstein, "For a History of Literary Property: John Wolfe's Reformation," *English Literary Renaissance* 18 (1988): 389–412; Mark Rose, "The Author as Proprietor: Donaldson v. Becket and the Genealogy of Modern Authorship," *Representations* 23 (1988): 51–85; and Woodmansee, "Genius and the Copyright," 425–48.

12. See Rogers, *Grub Street*, for the most complete study of the individuals involved.

13. D. N. Deluna, "Cotton Mather Published Abroad," *Early American Literature* 26 (1991): 153.

14. "Advertisement," Robert Fleming, *The Mirrour of Divine Love UnVail'd in a Poetical Paraphrase of the High and Mysterious Song of Solomon . . . A Miscellany of Several Other Poems* (London, 1691), sig. 215v.

15. "Robert Fleming the younger," in *The Dictionary of National Biography*. Concerning the dating of "Nature's Sermon," see Bodleian Library, MS Rawl.poet.213, 37r.

16. "John Salusbury," in *A Dictionary of the Printers and Booksellers who were at work in England, Scotland, and Ireland from 1669 to 1725*, ed. Henry R. Plomer (London: Bibliographical Society, 1968), 260.

17. Bodleian Library, MS Rawl.poet.213, 79r.

18. Margaret Cavendish, "The Epistle," in *The World's Olio* (London, 1655). I am indebted to Sally Moreman for pointing this example out to me.

19. Ralph Thoresby, *The Diary of Ralph Thoresby*, ed. Joseph Hunter, 2 vols. (London, 1830), 2:77.

20. Henry Plomer, introduction to *A Dictionary of the Booksellers and Printers Who Were at Work in England, Scotland, and Ireland from 1641 to 1667* (London: Bibliographical Society, 1968), xxiii.

21. Cotton Mather, *The Diary of Cotton Mather*, ed. Worthington Ford, *Collec-*

tions of the Massachusetts Historical Society, 7th ser., 7–8 (1912): 1:87.

22. In his account of Mather's connections with the Royal Society, David Levin omits the detail that Waller, as well as Woodward, received "Curiosa Americana"; Waller, who oversaw the production of the *Philosophical Transactions,* proposed Mather for the society in 1713. See Raymond P. Sterne, "Colonial Fellows of the Royal Society of London, 1661–1788," *Notes and Records of the Royal Society* 8 (1950): 178–246, and Margaret J. M. Ezell, "Richard Waller, S.R.S.: 'In the Pursuit of Nature,'" *Notes and Records of the Royal Society of London* 38 (1984): 215–33; on Mather's text, see David Levin, "Giants in the Earth: Science and the Occult in Cotton Mather's Letters to the Royal Society," *William and Mary Quarterly,* ser. 3, 45 (1988): 759.

23. Royal Society of London, MSS W.3, f. 75.

24. Raymond P. Sterne, "James Petiver," *American Antiquarian Society* (1952): 326–27.

25. Albert B. Cook, "Damaging the Mathers: London Receives the News from Salem," *New England Quarterly* 65 (1992): 303; see also T. J. Holmes, *Cotton Mather: A Bibliography of His Works,* 3 vols. (Cambridge: Harvard Univ. Press, 1940), and Deluna, "Cotton Mather," app. 2(a), 164–65, for illustrations of the two title pages, which differ slightly from Cook's representations of them in his article.

26. Bodleian Library, MS Rawl.D.72, f. 147r.

27. An interesting example of "the biter bit" can be seen with the production of Matthew Prior's collected poems in 1707 by Edmund Curll. As Curll's biographer Ralph Straus comments, "How these poems came into [Curll's] hands we do not known, but with two doubtful exceptions they were genuine." Prior's publisher, Jacob Tonson, published this statement in the *Daily Courant,* 24 January 1706/7: "This is to inform the World, that all the Genuine Copys of what Mr. Prior has hitherto written, do of right belong, and are now in the hands of Jacob Tonson, who intends very speedily to publish a correct Edition of them." Curll published his unauthorized edition in 1707, but Tonson's did not appear until late in 1708. Quoted in Straus, *Unspeakable Curll,* 21.

28. Royal Society MS, E.5, f. 6.

29. Mary Chudleigh, "To the Reader," in *Essays upon Several Subjects,* in *The Poems and Prose of Mary, Lady Chudleigh,* ed. Margaret J. M. Ezell (New York: Oxford Univ. Press, 1993), 248.

Chapter Five
Getting into Print

1. Notable exceptions to this trend are Maureen Bell, "Hannah Allen and the Development of a Puritan Publishing Business, 1646–1651," *Publishing History* 26 (1989): 5–66; Gerald MacLean, "Literacy, Class, and Gender in Restoration Eng-

land," *Text* 7 (1995): 307–35; and Paula McDowell, *The Women of Grub Street: Press, Politics, and Gender in the London Literary Marketplace, 1688–1730* (Oxford: Clarendon Press, 1997), which specifically investigate women's roles in the production of print texts.

2. W. H. Allnutt, "English Provincial Presses, Part III," *Bibliographica* 2 (1895): 296–97.

3. For details concerning the individual provincial printers listed, see Plomer, *Dictionary . . . from 1641 to 1667,* and Plomer, *A Dictionary of the Printers and Booksellers who were at work in England, Scotland and Ireland from 1668 to 1725* (London: Bibliographical Society, 1968). Concerning transient Civil War printers, see Allnutt, "English Provincial Presses," 280–97, for specific accounts of Royalist printers at work in these cities.

4. D. G. Vaisey, "Anthony Stephens: The Rise and Fall of an Oxford Bookseller," in *Studies in the Book Trade in Honour of Graham Pollard,* ed. R. W. Hunt, I. G. Philip, and R. J. Roberts (Oxford: Oxford Bibliographical Society, 1975), 95.

5. Robert Davies, *A Memoir of the York Press with Notices of Authors, Printers, and Stationers in the Sixteenth, Seventeenth, and Eighteenth Centuries* (London, 1868), 71–72, 89–97. See also entries for each in Henry R. Plomer, *A Dictionary of the Printers and Booksellers who were at work in England, Scotland, and Ireland, 1557–1640* (London: Bibliographical Society, 1968), 33.

6. See Plomer, *Dictionary . . . 1557–1640,* 38–39, and Davies, *Memoir,* 98–104, for details of Bulkley's numerous moves and trouble with the authorities.

7. James Maclehose, *The Glasgow University Press, 1638–1931* (Glasgow: Glasgow Univ. Press, 1931), 21.

8. See William J. Duncan, ed., *Notices and Documents Illustrative of the Literary History of Glasgow, During the Greater Part of the Last Century* (Glasgow, 1886), 2, for an account of Andrew Anderson's record as the printer for the University of Edinburgh.

9. James Watson, *The History of the Art of Printing, Containing an Account of Its Invention and Progress in Europe* (Edinburgh, 1713; reprint, London: Gregg Press, 1965), 12.

10. Ibid., 12–13; see also Paula Backscheider's more sympathetic account of Agnes Campbell Anderson in *Daniel Defoe: His Life* (Baltimore: Johns Hopkins Univ. Press, 1989), 305–7.

11. Robert Bowes, *A Catalogue of Books Printed at or Relating to the University Town and County of Cambridge from 1521 to 1893* (Cambridge, 1894).

12. Falconer Madan, *Oxford Books: A Bibliography of Printed Works Relating to the University and City of Oxford or Printed or Published There* (Oxford: Clarendon Press, 1931), vol. 3.

13. Morrice's manuscript is found in the Bodleian Library, MS Rawl.poet.114.

14. Foster, *Alumni Oxonienses,* 3:1035.

15. Bodleian Library, MS Rawl.poet.114, 2r. There is also a separate verse by him in MS Rawl.D.1145, 70v, "A Poem upon . . . the Difference between Real and Counterfeit Love."

16. Samuel Lewis, *Topographical Dictionary of Wales,* 3d ed. (London, 1845), 2:118–19.

17. Geraint H. Jenkins, *Literature, Religion, and Society in Wales, 1660–1730* (Cardiff: Univ. of Wales Press, 1978), 35.

18. J. C. Morrice, *A Manual of Welsh Literature* (Bangor, Wales, 1909), chap. 13. See also Morrice's *Wales in the Seventeenth Century: Its Literature and Men of Letters and Action* (Bangor, Wales, 1918), chaps. 2 and 3.

19. "Bulkeley Manuscripts, XII," *Archaeologia Cambrensis,* n.s., 3 (1852): 32.

Chapter Six
Making a Classic

I am grateful to the *South Central Review* for permission to reprint this essay. It appeared before I had the chance to benefit from Barbara Benedict's excellent study of the development of collections of literary "beauties" and anthologies of selected verse by publishers in the latter part of the eighteenth century, *Making the Modern Reader: Cultural Mediation in Early Modern Literary Anthologies* (Princeton: Princeton Univ. Press, 1996).

1. "Plan and Catalogue of Cooke's Uniform, Cheap, and Elegant Pocket Library" in James Thomson, *Works* (London, 1794), 3.

2. Samuel Johnson, ed., *A Dictionary of the English Language* (1755; reprint, London: Times Books, 1979), vol. 1, "Classick."

3. Following not far behind the term *classic* as a label for a particular type of text produced in a uniform format in a large series is *library.* Like *classic,* the designation *library* as part of a series label carries with it rich implications about the nature of the texts in the series. We have "Everyman Library," with the motto "Everyman, I will go with thee, and be thy guide, In thy most need to go by thy side"; the New American Library; and the Modern Library Edition when we sit down to select texts for class.

4. See Lyman Ray Patterson, *Copyright in Historical Perspective* (Nashville: Vanderbilt Univ. Press, 1968), chaps. 7 and 8; Frank Arthur Mumby and Ian Norrie, *Publishing and Bookselling,* 5th ed. rev. (London: Jonathan Cape, 1974), pt. 1, chaps. 8 and 9; Roy McKeen Wiles, *Serial Publication in England before 1750* (Cambridge: Cambridge Univ. Press, 1957), chaps. 3 and 5; Plant, *English Book Trade,* chaps. 5, 11, and 12.

5. Quoted in Mumby and Norrie, *Publishing and Bookselling,* 172.

6. Richard D. Altick, "From Aldine to Everyman: Cheap Reprint Series of the English Classics, 1830–1906," *Studies in Bibliography* 11 (1958): 7–8.

7. *A Collection of Poems By Several Hands. Most of them Written by Persons of Eminent Quality* (London, 1693), title page.

8. Dodsley's collection was expanded by Pearch in 1775 and then reedited by Isaac Reed in 1782. See William Prideaux Courtney's introduction to *Dodsley's Collection of Poetry: Its Contents and Contributors* (reprint, New York: Burt Franklin, 1968).

9. Robert Dodsley, "Preface to the First Edition," in *A Select Collection of Old Plays,* rev. Octavious Gilchrist and J. P. Collier (London, 1825), 1:xxix.

10. See Thomas F. Bonnell, "John Bell's *Poets of Great Britain:* The 'Little Trifling Edition' Revisited," *Modern Philology* 85 (1987): 128–52; Stanley Morison, *John Bell, 1745–1831: Bookseller, Printer, Publisher, Typefounder, Journalist, &c* (Cambridge: for the author at Cambridge Univ. Press, 1930); and William J. Cameron, *John Bell's Edition of the "The Poets of Great Britain (1777–1793),* WHSTC Bibliography, no. 15 (London, Ontario: Western Ontario Univ., 1983).

11. *Morning Post* (13 January 1775), 1.

12. Advertisement, in *Bell's British Theatre* (London, 1776), 1:[1–3].

13. Printed in Morison, *John Bell,* 37.

Works Cited

Manuscript Collections
The Bodleian Library
The British Library
The Folger Shakespeare Library
The Henry E. Huntington Library
The Royal Society of London

Primary and Secondary Works

Achinstein, Sharon. *Milton and the Revolutionary Reader*. Princeton: Princeton Univ. Press, 1994.

A Collection of Poems by Several Hands. Most of them Written by Persons of Eminent Quality. London, 1693.

Allnutt, W. H. "English Provincial Presses, Part III." *Bibliographica* 2 (1895): 276–308.

Altick, Richard D. "From Aldine to Everyman: Cheap Reprint Series of the English Classics, 1830–1906." *Studies in Bibliography* 11 (1958): 3–24.

Amore, Adelaide P. *A Woman's Inner World: Selected Prose and Poetry of Anne Bradstreet*. Lanham, Md.: Univ. Press of America, 1982.

Andreadis, Harriette. "The Sapphic-Platonics of Katherine Philips, 1632–1664." *Signs* 15 (1989): 34–60.

Ault, Norman. *New Light on Pope with Some Additions to His Poetry Hitherto Unknown*. London: Methuen, 1949.

Backscheider, Paula. *Daniel Defoe: His Life*. Baltimore: Johns Hopkins Univ. Press, 1989.

Barker, Jane. *The Galesia Trilogy and Selected Manuscript Poems*. Edited by Carol Shiner Wilson. New York: Oxford Univ. Press, 1997.

Beal, Peter. "Notations in Garrison: The Seventeenth-Century Commonplace Book." In *New Ways of Looking at Old Texts*, edited by W. Speed Hill, 131–47. Binghamton, N.Y.: Renaissance Text Society, 1993.

————, ed. *Index of English Literary Manuscripts, 1500–1800.* New York: Bowker, 1980–.

Belanger, Terry. "Publishers and Writers in Eighteenth-Century England." In *Books and Their Readers in Eighteenth-Century England,* edited by Isabel Rivers, 5–25. London: St. Martin's Press, 1982.

Bell, Maureen. "Hannah Allen and the Development of a Puritan Publishing Business, 1646–1651." *Publishing History* 26 (1989): 5–66.

Bell's British Theatre. London, 1776.

Benedict, Barbara. *Making the Modern Reader: Cultural Mediation in Early Modern Literary Anthologies.* Princeton: Princeton Univ. Press, 1996.

Bennett, H. S. *English Books and Readers, 1603 to 1640.* Cambridge: Cambridge Univ. Press, 1970.

Black, Jeremy. *The English Press in the Eighteenth Century.* Philadelphia: Univ. of Pennsylvania Press, 1987.

Blagden, Cyprian. *The Stationers Company: A History, 1403–1959.* Cambridge: Harvard Univ. Press, 1960.

Bloom, Edward. "Samuel Johnson on Copyright." *Journal of English and German Philology* 47 (1948): 165–72.

Bonnell, Thomas F. "John Bell's *Poets of Great Britain*: The 'Little Trifling Edition' Revisited." *Modern Philology* 85 (1987): 128–52.

Bossy, John. *The English Catholic Community, 1579–1850.* London: Darton, 1975.

Bowes, Robert. *A Catalogue of Books Printed at or Relating to the University Town and County of Cambridge from 1521 to 1893.* Cambridge, 1894.

Bowker, R. R. *Copyright: Its History and Law.* Boston: Houghton Mifflin, 1912.

Bradstreet, Anne. *The Tenth Muse.* London, 1650.

————. *The Works of Anne Bradstreet in Prose and Verse.* Edited by J. H. Ellis. 1867. Fasc. ed., Glouster, Mass.: P. Smith, 1962.

Brown, Nancy Pollard. "Paperchase: The Dissemination of Catholic Texts in Elizabethan England." *English Manuscript Studies, 1100–1700* 1 (1989): 120–43.

"Bulkeley Manuscripts, XII." *Archeologia Cambrensis,* n.s., 3 (1852): 31–35.

Burke, Victoria Elizabeth. "Women and Early Seventeenth-Century Manuscript Culture: Four Miscellanies." *Seventeenth Century* 12 (1997): 135–50.

————. "Women and Seventeenth-Century Manuscript Culture: Miscellanies, Commonplace Books, and Song Books Compiled by English and Scottish Women, 1600–1660." Ph.D. diss., Oxford University, 1996.

Butt, John. "Pope's Poetical Manuscripts." In *Essential Articles for the Study of Alexander Pope,* edited by Maynard Mack, 545–65. Rev. ed. Hamden, Conn.: Archon Books, 1968.

Cameron, William J. *John Bell's Edition of the "Poets of Great Britain" (1777–1793).* WHSTC Bibliography, n. 15. London, Ontario: Western Ontario Univ., 1983.

Carnie, Robert Hay. "Scottish Printers and Booksellers, 1668–1775: A Second Supplement (I)." *Studies in Bibliography* 14 (1961): 81–96.

———. "Scottish Printers and Booksellers, 1668–1775: A Second Supplement (II)." *Studies in Bibliography* 15 (1962): 105–20.

Carnie, Robert Hay, and Ronald Paterson Doig. "Scottish Printers and Booksellers, 1668–1775: A Supplement." *Studies in Bibliography* 12 (1959): 130–59.

Cary, Patrick. *The Poems of Patrick Cary.* Edited by Sister Veronica Delaney. Oxford: Clarendon Press, 1978.

Cavendish, Margaret. *The World's Olio.* London, 1655.

Chartier, Roger. *The Order of Books.* Translated by Lydia G. Cochrane. Stanford: Stanford Univ. Press, 1994.

Chudleigh, Mary. *The Poems and Prose of Mary, Lady Chudleigh.* Edited by Margaret J. M. Ezell. New York: Oxford Univ. Press, 1993.

Clerk, Sir John. *Memoirs of the Life of Sir John Clerk of Penicuik, Baronet.* Edited by John M. Gay. Edinburgh, 1892.

Clifford, Arthur, ed. *Tixall Letters.* 2 vols. Edinburgh, 1815.

———, ed. *Tixall Poetry.* Edinburgh, 1813.

Cook, Albert B. "Damaging the Mathers: London Receives the News from Salem." *New England Quarterly* 65 (1992): 302–8.

Cooke, John. "Plan and Catalogue of Cooke's Uniform, Cheap, and Elegant Pocket Library." In *James Thomason, Works.* London, 1794.

Courtney, William Prideaux, ed. *Dodsley's Collection of Poetry: Its Contents and Contributors.* 1910. Reprint, New York: Burt Franklin, 1968.

Cressy, David. "Literacy in Context: Meaning and Measurements in Early Modern England." In *Consumption and the World of Goods,* edited by John Brewer and Roy Porter, 305–19. London: Routledge, 1993.

Culliton, Barbara J. "Stanford President Calls for New Authorship Policy." *Science* 230 (1985): 422–23.

Davies, Robert. *A Memoir of the York Press with Notices of Authors, Printers, and Stationers in the Sixteenth, Seventeenth, and Eighteenth Centuries.* London, 1868.

Deluna, D. N. "Cotton Mather Published Abroad." *Early American Literature* 26 (1991): 145–72.

Dobrée, Bonamy. *English Literature in the Early Eighteenth Century, 1700–1740.* Oxford: Clarendon Press, 1959.

Dodsley, Robert, ed. *A Select Collection of Old Plays.* Revised by Octavious Gilchrist and J. P. Collier. 12 vols. London, 1825.

Dryden, John. *The Letters of John Dryden.* Edited by Charles E. Ward. Durham, N.C.: Duke Univ. Press, 1942.

Duncan, William J., ed. *Notices and Documents Illustrative of the Literary History of Glasgow, During the Greater Part of the Last Century.* Glasgow, 1886.

Duncan-Jones, Katherine. *Sir Philip Sidney: Courtier Poet*. New Haven: Yale Univ. Press, 1991.

———. *Sir Philip Sidney: Life, Death, and Legend*. Oxford: Clarendon Press, 1986.

Dunton, John. *The Life and Errors of John Dunton . . . to which are added Selections from his Other Genuine Works*. 2 vols. 1818. Reprint, New York: Burt Franklin, 1969.

Eisenstein, Elizabeth. *The Printing Press as an Agent of Change*. Cambridge: Cambridge Univ. Press, 1980.

Erskine-Hill, Howard. "Alexander Pope at Fifteen: A New Manuscript." *Review of English Studies*, n.s., 18 (1966): 268–77.

———. "Under Which Caesar? Pope in the Journal of Mrs. Charles Caesar." *Review of English Studies*, n.s., 33 (1982): 436–44.

Evans, Arise. *A Voice from Heaven*. London, 1652.

Evans, Willa McClung. *Henry Lawes: Musician and Friend of Poets*. New York: Modern Language Association, 1941.

Ezell, Margaret J. M. "The *Gentleman's Journal* and the Commercialization of Restoration Coterie Literary Practices." *Modern Philology* 89 (1992): 323–40.

———. *The Patriarch's Wife: Literary Evidence and the History of the Family*. Chapel Hill: Univ. of North Carolina Press, 1987.

———. "Richard Waller, S.R.S.: 'In the Pursuit of Nature.'" *Notes and Records of the Royal Society of London* 38 (1984): 215–33.

———. "'To Be Your Daughter in Your Pen': The Social Functions of Literature in the Writings of Lady Elizabeth Brackley and Lady Jane Cavendish." *Huntington Library Quarterly* 51 (1988): 281–96.

———. *Writing Women's Literary History*. Baltimore: Johns Hopkins Univ. Press, 1993.

Feather, John. *The Provincial Book Trade in Eighteenth-Century England*. Cambridge: Cambridge Univ. Press, 1985.

Fleming, Robert. *The Mirrour of Divine Love UnVail'd in a Poetical Paraphrase of the High and Mysterious Song of Solomon . . . A Miscellany of Several Other Poems*. London, 1691.

Foster, Joseph. *Alumni Oxonienses: The Members of the University of Oxford, 1500–1714*. 1891. Reprint, 4 vols., Nendeln, Liechtenstein: Kraus Reprint, 1968.

Foucault, Michel. "What Is an Author?" In *Critical Theory since 1965*, edited by Hazard Adams and Leroy Searle, 138–48. Tallahassee: Univ. of Florida Press, 1992.

Fox, Adam. "Popular Verses and Their Readership in the Early Seventeenth Century." In Raven, Small, and Tadmor, *Practice and Representation of Reading in England*, 125–37.

Foxon, David. *Pope and the Early Eighteenth-Century Book Trade*. Rev. ed. by James McLaverty. Oxford: Clarendon Press, 1991.

Freeman, Phyllis. "Two Fragments of Walsh Manuscripts." *Review of English Studies,* n.s., 8 (1957): 390–401.

———. "William Walsh and Dryden: Recently Recovered Letters." *Review of English Studies* 24 (1948): 195–202.

Friedman, Jerome. *The Battle of the Frogs and Fairford's Flies: Miracles and the Pulp Press during the English Revolution.* New York: St. Martin's Press, 1993.

Furet, François. *In the Workshop of History.* Translated by Jonathan Mandelbaum. Chicago: Univ. of Chicago Press, 1984.

Giles, Peter. "An Unknown Emmanuel Poet." *Emmanuel College Magazine* 9 (1897): 1–22.

Goreau, Angeline. *Reconstructing Aphra: A Social Biography of Aphra Behn.* Oxford: Clarendon Press, 1980.

Greg, W. W. *Some Aspects and Problems of London Publishing between 1550 and 1650.* Oxford: Clarendon Press, 1956.

Griffin, Dustin. "Fictions of Eighteenth-Century Authorship." *Essays in Criticism* 43 (1993): 181–94.

Grundy, Isobel. "The Politics of Female Authorship: Lady Mary Wortley Montagu's Reaction to the Printing of Her Poems." *Book Collector* 31 (1982): 19–37.

Grusin, Richard. "What Is an Electronic Author: Theory and Technological Fallacy." *Configurations* 3 (1994): 469–83.

Hageman, Elizabeth. "Making a Good Impression: Early Texts and Letters by Katherine Philips." *South Central Review* 11 (1994): 39–65.

Hageman, Elizabeth, and Andrea Sununu. "New Manuscript Texts of Katherine Philips, the Matchless Orinda." *English Manuscript Studies, 1100–1700* 4 (1993): 174–219.

Halsband, Robert. *The Life of Lady Mary Wortley Montagu.* London: Oxford Univ. Press, 1956.

———. "Pope, Lady Mary, and the Court Poems." *PMLA* 68 (1953): 237–50.

Handover, P. M. *Printing in London from 1476 to Modern Times.* Cambridge: Harvard Univ. Press, 1960.

Harris, Brice. "Captain Robert Julian, Secretary to the Muses." *ELH* 10 (1943): 294–309.

Hobbs, Mary, "Early Seventeenth-Century Verse Miscellanies and Their Value for Textual Editors." *English Manuscript Studies, 1100–1700* 1 (1989): 182–210.

Holmes, T. J. *Cotton Mather: A Bibliography of His Works.* 3 vols. Cambridge: Harvard Univ. Press, 1940.

Jackson, Thomas, ed. "The Life of Elizabeth Singer Rowe." In *Library of Christian Biography,* 10:185–275. London, 1839.

Jenkins, Geraint H. *Literature, Religion, and Society in Wales, 1660–1730.* Cardiff: Univ. of Wales Press, 1978.

Johnson, Samuel. *A Dictionary of the English Language.* 2 vols. 1755. Reprint, London: Times Books, 1979.

Judge, Cyril Bathurst. *Elizabethan Book Pirates.* Cambridge: Harvard Univ. Press, 1934.

Kernan, Alvin. *Samuel Johnson and the Impact of Print.* Princeton: Princeton Univ. Press, 1987.

Kerrigan, John. "The Editor as Reader." In Raven, Small, and Tadmore, *Practice and Representation of Reading in England,* 102–24.

King, Henry. *Poems, Elegies.* London, 1657.

King, Kathryn R. "Jane Barker, *Poetical Recreations,* and the Sociable Text." *ELH* 61 (1994): 551–70.

King, Kathryn R., and Jeslyn Medoff. "Jane Barker and Her Life (1652–1732): The Documentary Record." *Eighteenth-Century Life* 21 (1997): 16–38.

Kirschbaum, Leo. "Authors' Copyright in England before 1640." *Publications of the Bibliographical Society of America* 40 (1946): 43–80.

Klancher, Jon P. *The Making of English Reading Audiences, 1790–1832.* Madison: Univ. of Wisconsin Press, 1987.

Kraus, Kari Michelle. "The Wit Restor'd; or, The Critics' Rejoinder: A Revaluation of William Walsh." M.A. thesis, Texas A&M University, 1995.

LaBelle, Jenijoy. "The Huntington Aston Manuscript." *Book Collector* 29 (1980): 542–67.

———. "A True Love's Knot: The Letters of Constance Fowler and the Poems of Herbert Aston." *Journal of English and Germanic Philology* 79 (1980): 13–31.

Landow, George. *Hypertext.* Baltimore: Johns Hopkins Univ. Press, 1992.

Lawes, Henry. *Ayres and Dialogues.* London, 1653.

Lerner, Joshua. "Science and Agricultural Progress: Quantitative Evidence from England, 1660–1780." *Agricultural History* 66 (1992): 11–27.

Levin, David. "Giants in the Earth: Science and the Occult in Cotton Mather's Letters to the Royal Society." *William and Mary Quarterly,* ser. 3, 45 (1988): 751–70.

Lewis, Samuel. *Topographical Dictionary of Wales.* 3d ed. 2 vols. London, 1845.

Limbert, Claudia A. "Katherine Philips: Controlling a Life and Reputation." *South Atlantic Review* 56 (1991): 27–42.

Long, Pamela O. "Invention, Authorship, 'Intellectual Property,' and the Origin of Patents: Notes toward a Conceptual History." *Technology and Culture* 32 (1991): 846–84.

Love, Harold. *Scribal Publication in Seventeenth-Century England.* London: Oxford Univ. Press, 1993.

Lowenstein, Joseph. "For a History of Literary Property: John Wolfe's Reformation." *English Literary Renaissance* 18 (1988): 389–412.

———. "The Script in the Marketplace." *Representations* 12 (1985): 101–14.

Lynch, Kathleen. *Jacob Tonson, Kit-Cat Publisher.* Knoxville: Univ. of Tennessee Press, 1971.

MacColl, Alan. "The Circulation of Donne's Poems in Manuscript." In *John Donne: Essays in Celebration,* edited by A. J. Smith, 28–46. London: Methuen, 1972.

MacDermott, Kathy. "Literature and the Grub Street Myth." *Literature and History* 8 (1982): 159–69.

Mack, Maynard. *Alexander Pope: A Life.* New York: Norton, 1985.

MacLean, Gerald. "Literacy, Class, and Gender in Restoration England." *Text* 7 (1995): 307–35.

Maclehose, James. *The Glasgow University Press, 1638–1931.* Glasgow: Glasgow Univ. Press, 1931.

Madan, Falconer. *Oxford Books: A Bibliography of Printed Works Relating to the University and City of Oxford or Printed or Published There.* 3 vols. Oxford: Clarendon Press, 1931.

Mambretti, Catherine Cole. "Fugitive Papers: A New Orinda Poem and Problems in Her Canon." *Publications of the Bibliographical Society of America* 71 (1977): 443–52.

Marcus, Stephen. "Reading, Writing, and Hypertext." *College Literature* 15 (1988): 9–18.

Marotti, Arthur F. *Manuscript, Print, and the English Renaissance Lyric.* Ithaca, N.Y.: Cornell Univ. Press, 1995.

Martin, Henri-Jean. *The History and Power of Writing.* Translated by Lydia G. Cochrane. Chicago: Univ. of Chicago Press, 1994.

Martin, L. C. "A Forgotten Poet of the Seventeenth Century." *Essays and Studies* 11 (1925): 5–31.

Mather, Cotton. *The Diary of Cotton Mather.* Edited by Worthington Ford. 2 vols. *Collections of the Massachusetts Historical Society,* 7th ser., 7–8 (1912).

May, Steven W. *The Elizabethan Courtier Poets: The Poems and Their Contexts.* Columbia: Univ. of Missouri Press, 1991.

———. "Tudor Aristocrats and the Mythical 'Stigma of Print.'" *Renaissance Papers* 10 (1980): 11–18.

McDowell, Paula. *The Women of Grub Street: Press, Politics, and Gender in the London Literary Marketplace, 1688–1730.* Oxford: Clarendon Press, 1997.

McGann, Jerome. "The Text, the Poem, and the Problem of Historical Method." In *The Beauty of Inflections: Literary Investigations in Historical Method and Theory,* 111–32. Oxford: Clarendon Press, 1985.

McLaverty, James. "The First Printing and Publication of Pope's Letters." *Library* 2 (1980): 264–80.

Mendelson, Sara Heller. "Stuart Women's Diaries." In *Women in English Society, 1500–1800,* edited by Mary Prior, 181–210. London: Methuen, 1985.

Mermin, Dorothy. "Women Becoming Poets: Katherine Philips, Anne Finch, Aphra Behn." *ELH* 57 (1990): 335–55.

Miner, Earl. *The Cavalier Modes from Jonson to Cotton.* Princeton: Princeton Univ. Press, 1971.

Mollineux, Mary. *Fruits of Retirement.* London, 1702.

Montagu, Lady Mary Wortley. *The Complete Letters.* Edited by Robert Halsband. 3 vols. Oxford: Clarendon Press, 1965–67.

Morison, Stanley. *John Bell, 1745–1831: Bookseller, Printer, Publisher, Typefounder, Journalist, &c.* Cambridge: for the author at Cambridge Univ. Press, 1930.

Morrice, J. C. *A Manual of Welsh Literature.* Bangor, Wales: Jarvis & Foster, 1909.

———. *Wales in the Seventeenth Century: Its Literature and Men of Letters and Action.* Bangor, Wales: Jarvis & Foster, 1918.

Mumby, Frank Arthur, and Ian Norrie. *Publishing and Bookselling.* 5th ed. rev. London: Jonathan Cape, 1974.

Nichols, John. *The History and Antiquities of the County of Leicester.* 4 vols. 2d ed. London, 1813.

The Norton Anthology of English Literature. 2 vols. 6th ed. New York: Norton, 1993.

Parks, Stephen. *John Dunton and the English Book Trade: A Study of His Career with a Checklist of His Publications.* New York: Garland Publishing, 1976.

Pask, Kevin. *The Emergence of the English Author: Scripting the Life of the Poet in Early Modern England.* Cambridge: Cambridge Univ. Press, 1996.

Patterson, Lyman Ray. *Copyright in Historical Perspective.* Nashville: Vanderbilt Univ. Press, 1968.

Perkins, David. *Is Literary History Possible?* Baltimore: Johns Hopkins Univ. Press, 1992.

Peters, Julie Stone. *Congreve, the Drama, and the Printed Word.* Stanford: Stanford Univ. Press, 1990.

Philips, Katherine. *The Collected Works of Katherine Philips, the Matchless Orinda.* Edited by Patrick Thomas. 3 vols. Essex: Stump Cross Press, 1990.

———. *Letters from Orinda to Poliarchus.* London, 1705.

Plant, Marjorie. *The English Book Trade: An Economic History of the Making and Sale of Books.* 3d ed. London: George Allen & Unwin, 1974.

Plomer, Henry R. *A Dictionary of the Booksellers and Printers Who Were at Work in England, Scotland, and Ireland from 1641 to 1667.* London: Bibliographical Society, 1968.

———. *A Dictionary of the Printers and Booksellers who were at work in England, Scotland, and Ireland, 1557–1640.* London: Bibliographical Society, 1968.

———. *A Dictionary of the Printers and Booksellers Who Were at Work in England,*

Scotland, and Ireland from 1669 to 1725. London: Bibliographical Society, 1968.

Pollard, M. *Dublin's Trade in Books, 1550–1800*. Oxford: Clarendon Press, 1989.

Pope, Alexander. *The Correspondence*. Edited by George Sherburn. 5 vols. Oxford: Clarendon Press, 1956.

———. *The Prose Works of Alexander Pope*. Vol. 1. Edited by Norman Ault. Oxford: Basil Blackwell, 1936.

———. *The Prose Works of Alexander Pope*. Vol. 2. Edited by Rosemary Cowler. Hamden, Conn.: Archon Books, 1986.

Powell, Walter W. *Getting into Print: The Decision-Making Process in Scholarly Publishing*. Chicago: Univ. of Chicago Press, 1985.

Quarles, Francis. *Judgment and Mercie for Afflicted Souls*. London, 1646.

Randall, Dale B. J. *Gentle Flame: The Life and Verse of Dudley, Fourth Lord North (1602–1677)*. Durham, N.C.: Duke Univ. Press, 1983.

Ransom, Harry. *The First Copyright Statute*. Austin: Univ. of Texas Press, 1956.

———. "The Rewards of Authorship in the Eighteenth Century." *University of Texas Studies in English* 18 (1938): 47–66.

Raven, James, Helen Small, and Naomi Tadmor, eds. *The Practice and Representation of Reading in England*. Cambridge: Cambridge Univ. Press, 1996.

Rogers, Pat. *Grub Street: Studies in a Subculture*. London: Methuen, 1972.

———. "Pope and His Subscribers." *Publishing History* 3 (1978): 7–36.

Rose, Jonathan. "Rereading the English Common Reader: A Preface to a History of Audiences." *Journal of the History of Ideas* 53 (1992): 47–70.

Rose, Mark. "The Author as Proprietor: Donaldson v. Becket and the Genealogy of Modern Authorship." *Representations* 23 (1988): 51–85.

———. *Authors and Owners: The Invention of Copyright*. Cambridge: Harvard Univ. Press, 1993.

Rosenmeier, Rosamond. *Anne Bradstreet Revisited*. Boston: Twayne Publishers, 1991.

Rostenberg, Leona. *Literary, Political, Scientific, Religious, and Legal Publishing, Printing, and Bookselling in England, 1551–1700: Twelve Studies*. 2 vols. New York: Burt Franklin, 1965.

Sanders, J. W. "The Stigma of Print: A Note on the Social Bases of Tudor Poetry." *Essays in Criticism* 1 (1951): 139–64.

Saunders, David, and Ian Hunter. "Lessons from the 'Literary': How to Historicize Authorship." *Critical Inquiry* 17 (1991): 479–509.

Sherburn, George. *The Early Career of Alexander Pope*. Oxford: Clarendon Press, 1934.

Small, Christopher. *The Printed Word: An Instrument of Popularity*. Aberdeen, Scotland: Aberdeen Univ. Press, 1982.

Smith, Nigel. *Literature and Revolution in England, 1640–1660*. New Haven: Yale Univ. Press, 1994.

Spence, Joseph. *Anecdotes, Observations, and Characters of Books and Men.* Edited by Samuel Weller Singer. Introduction by Bonamy Dobrée. 1819. Reprint, Carbondale: Southern Illinois Press, 1964.

Spufford, Margaret. "First Steps in Literacy: The Reading and Writing Experiences of the Humblest Seventeenth-Century Spiritual Autobiographers." *Social History* 4 (1979): 407–35.

———. *Small Books and Pleasant Histories.* Athens: Univ. of Georgia Press, 1981.

Sterne, Raymond P. "Colonial Fellows of the Royal Society of London, 1661–1788." *Notes and Records of the Royal Society* 8 (1950): 178–246.

———. "James Petiver." *American Antiquarian Society* (October 1952): 326–27.

Straus, Ralph. *The Unspeakable Curll: Being Some Account of the Life of Edmund Curll, Bookseller.* London: Chapman and Hall, 1927.

Sussman, Marvin B. "The Charybdis of Publishing in Academia." *Marriage and Family Review* 18 (1993): 161–69.

Sutherland, James. *English Literature of the Late Seventeenth Century.* Oxford: Clarendon Press, 1969.

Taine, Hippolyte. *History of English Literature.* Translated by N. Van Laun. New York: William L. Allison Co., 1895.

Tanselle, G. Thomas. "Printing History and Other History." *Studies in Bibliography* 48 (1995): 269–89.

Taubes, Gary. "Electronic Preprints Point the Way to 'Author Empowerment.'" *Science* 271 (1996): 767–68.

Thomas, Keith. "The Meaning of Literacy in Early Modern England." In *The Written Word: Literacy in Transition,* edited by Gerd Bauman, 97–131. Oxford: Oxford Univ. Press, 1986.

Thoresby, Ralph. *The Diary of Ralph Thoresby.* Edited by Joseph Hunter. 2 vols. London, 1830.

Tinker, Nathan P. "John Grismond: Printer of the Unauthorized Edition of Katherine Philips's *Poems* (1664)." *English Language Notes* 34 (1996): 3–35.

Tribble, Evelyn B. *Margins and Marginality: The Printed Page in Early Modern England.* Charlottesville: Univ. Press of Virginia, 1993.

Uphaus, Robert W., and Gretchen M. Foster, eds. *The Other Eighteenth Century: English Women of Letters, 1660–1800.* East Lansing, Mich.: Colleagues Press, 1991.

Vaisey, D. G. "Anthony Stephens: The Rise and Fall of an Oxford Bookseller." In *Studies in the Book Trade in Honour of Graham Pollard,* edited by R. W. Hunt, I. G. Philip, and R. J. Jones, 91–117. Oxford: Oxford Bibliographical Society, 1975.

Vieth, David. *Attribution in Restoration Poetry.* New Haven: Yale Univ. Press, 1963.

Wall, Wendy. *The Imprint of Gender: Authorship and Publication in the English Renaissance.* Ithaca, N.Y.: Cornell Univ. Press, 1993.

Wanley, Nathaniel. *Poems.* Edited by L. C. Martin. Oxford: Clarendon Press, 1928.

Ward, Charles E. "The Publication and Profits of Dryden's *Virgil.*" *PMLA* 53 (1938): 807–12.

Watson, James. *The History of the Art of Printing, Containing an Account of Its Invention and Progress in Europe.* Edinburgh, 1713. Reprint, London: Gregg Press, 1965.

Watt, Ian. "Publishers and Sinners: The Augustan View." *Studies in Bibliography* 12 (1958): 3–20.

W[eaver], T[homas]. *Songs and Poems of Love and Drollery.* London, 1654.

Wedgwood, C. V. *Seventeenth-Century English Literature.* New York: Oxford Univ. Press, 1950.

White, Elizabeth Wade. *Anne Bradstreet: "The Tenth Muse."* New York: Oxford Univ. Press, 1971.

Wiles, Roy McKeen. *Serial Publication in England before 1750.* Cambridge: Cambridge Univ. Press, 1957.

Winn, James A. *John Dryden and His World.* New Haven: Yale Univ. Press, 1987.

———. "On Pope, Printers, and Publishers." *Eighteenth-Century Life* 6 (1981): 93–102.

———. *A Window in the Bosom.* Hamden, Conn.: Archon Books, 1977.

Wolf, Edwin, II. *The Book Culture of a Colonial American City.* Oxford: Clarendon Press, 1988.

———. *The Library of James Logan of Philadelphia, 1674–1751.* Philadelphia: Library Company of Philadelphia, 1974.

Wollman, Richard B. "The 'Press and the Fire': Print and MSS Culture in Donne's Circle." *Studies in English Literature, 1599–1900* 33 (1993): 85–97.

Woodmansee, Martha. "The Genius and the Copyright: Economic and Legal Conditions of the Emergence of the 'Author.'" *Eighteenth-Century Studies* 17 (1984): 425–48.

Woudhuysen, H. R. *Sir Philip Sidney and the Circulation of Manuscripts, 1558–1640.* Oxford: Clarendon Press, 1996.

Index

LIBRARY OF CONGRESS CATALOGING-IN-PUBLICATION DATA
Ezell, Margaret J. M.
    Social authorship and the advent of print / Margaret J. M. Ezell.
        p.   cm.
    Includes bibliographical references and index.
    ISBN 0-8018-6139-x (alk. paper)
    1. English literature—Early modern, 1500–1700—History and
criticism. 2. Authorship—Social aspects—Great Britain—History—
17th century. 3. Authorship—Social aspects—Great Britain—History—18th century. 4. Literature and society—Great Britain—
History—17th century. 5. Literature and society—Great Britain—
History—18th century. 6. English literature—18th century—History and criticism. 7. Literature publishing—Great Britain—History. 8. Printing—Great Britain—History.   I. Title.
PR438.S63E94   1999
820.9'004—dc21   98-49483
                                                                   CIP